New

A gift from the P.I.A,
the Parent involvement group
to the
Seven Hills School Library
December, 1996.

A
KWANZAA
CELEBRATION

A
KWANZAA
CELEBRATION

FESTIVE RECIPES AND
HOMEMADE GIFTS
FROM AN AFRICAN-AMERICAN
KITCHEN

Angela Shelf Medearis

A DUTTON BOOK

DUTTON
Published by the Penguin Group
Penguin Books USA Inc., 375 Hudson Street,
New York, New York 10014, U.S.A.
Penguin Books Ltd, 27 Wrights Lane,
London W8 5TZ, England
Penguin Books Australia Ltd, Ringwood,
Victoria, Australia
Penguin Books Canada Ltd, 10 Alcorn Avenue,
Toronto, Ontario, Canada M4V 3B2
Penguin Books (N.Z.) Ltd, 182–190 Wairau Road,
Auckland 10, New Zealand

Penguin Books Ltd, Registered Offices:
Harmondsworth, Middlesex, England

First published by Dutton, an imprint of Dutton Signet, a division
of Penguin Books USA Inc.
Distributed in Canada by McClelland & Stewart Inc.

First Printing, December, 1995
10 9 8 7 6 5 4 3 2 1

 REGISTERED TRADEMARK — MARCA REGISTRADA

Library of Congress Cataloging-in-Publication Data

Medearis, Angela Shelf.
    A Kwanzaa celebration : festive recipes and homemade gifts from an
    African-American kitchen / Angela Shelf Medearis.
        p. cm.
    ISBN 0-525-94070-7
    1. Afro-American cookery.   2. Holiday cookery — United States.
    3. Kwanzaa. I. Title.
    TX715.M483   1995
    641.59'296073 — dc20   95-33015
                                                        CIP

Printed in the United States of America
Set in Primer
Designed by Stanley S. Drate/Folio Graphics Co., Inc.

To my ancestors; my wonderful family, especially my husband, Michael, my daughter, Deanna, and my grandchild, Anysa, who are always ready to help in any way they can; and to Carole DeSanti and Julia Moskin, two of the best Yankee editors a Southerner could have. Thanks for believing in me.

A.S.M.

CONTENTS

PREFACE

More than twenty years ago, an African-American holiday was born. Its founder, Dr. Maulana Karenga, added an "a" to the Swahili word *kwanza,* which means "first fruits," to link the new holiday with its ancient past. I wrote this cookbook because I wanted to contribute to a celebration that was created by and for African-Americans. I also wanted to pay tribute to the contributions Africans and African-Americans have made to the world as chefs and culinary artists. To that end, I've compiled 100 favorite recipes with either history behind them or a unique tie to the Kwanzaa celebration.

Kwanzaa has its roots in the turmoil of the Watts riot of 1965. Not only did that riot reshape the African-American community in California, but it also had a profound effect on Dr. Karenga, who was a graduate student during that time. In 1966 Karenga received his doctorate and began teaching African-American history; he also began searching for ways to bring African-Americans together as a people and as a community. He founded US, a cultural organization, and started to research African Kwanza celebrations.

Dr. Karenga combined aspects of several different tribal harvest celebrations, from those of the Ashanti to those of the Zulu, to form the basis of Kwanzaa. Kwanzaa is not a religious holiday but a cultural celebration, observed from December 26 to January 1. Its goal is to help African-Americans define and unify themselves as a people, to further understanding of African culture, and to avoid the unfortunate commercialism of the American Christmas. Some African-Americans celebrate Christmas and Kwanzaa. Others choose to celebrate only Kwanzaa.

In Africa, "Kwanza" was a celebration held after the crops had been harvested. Our ancestors gathered together at a community feast to give thanks for the bountiful harvest and to celebrate the fruits of their labors with a wonderful meal. Many of the recipes in this cookbook have a traditional or historic tie with our African roots and with the rich culinary tradition our ancestors brought from Africa to America.

Whether you are searching for information to start a Kwanzaa celebration in your home for the first time, or whether you've celebrated Kwanzaa since its inception in 1966, this is the book for you.

Information and recipes to assist you with your celebration, including a step-by-step guide on how to celebrate each day of the seven-day holiday, are the heart of *A Kwanzaa Celebration*. I've also included a "Cooking for Company" chapter to help you prepare simple, delicious meals for large parties and/or the community suppers that are a popular part of the celebration.

The "Gifts from the Kitchen" chapter contains suggestions and recipes for easy-to-make *zawadi* gifts, the presents that are exchanged on January 1, the last day of Kwanzaa.

A Kwanzaa Celebration is my *zawadi* gift to you. May your Kwanzaa celebration be one that will unite you with our past, fortify you for the present, and prepare you for the future. *Harambee!* Let's pull together. *Kwanzaa yenu iwe na heri* (Happy Kwanzaa).

Angela Shelf Medearis
AUSTIN, TEXAS
MAY 1995

THE NGUZO SABA—
THE SEVEN PRINCIPLES

Dr. Karenga established this set of common goals for inspiration during Kwanzaa and as a guide for the African-American community all year long. These are the *nguzo saba* principles:

UMOJA *(Unity)*: To strive for and maintain unity in the family, community, nation, and the world African community.

KUJICHAGULIA *(Self-determination)*: To define ourselves, name ourselves, create for ourselves, and speak for ourselves instead of being defined, named, created for, and spoken for by others.

UJIMA *(Collective Work and Responsibility)*: To build and maintain our community together and to make our sisters' and brothers' problems our problems and to solve them together.

UJAMAA *(Cooperative Economics)*: To build and maintain our own stores, shops, and other businesses, and to profit from them together.

NIA *(Purpose):* To make our collective vocation the building and developing of our community in order to restore our people to their traditional greatness.

KUUMBA *(Creativity):* To do always as much as we can, in the way we can, in order to leave our community more beautiful and beneficial than it was when we inherited it.

IMANI *(Faith):* To believe with all our heart in our people, our parents, our teachers, our leaders, and the righteousness and victory of our struggle for a new and better world.

INTRODUCTION

A Recipe for Celebrating Kwanzaa

Every family's and community's Kwanzaa celebration is different. Whether you celebrate with three or thirty, the opportunity for reflection and recommitment is the same. As well as celebrating the unity of the African-American community, Kwanzaa celebrates our creativity and diversity. That's why you should remember that the guidelines below are just that—guidelines. Kwanzaa is a holiday that is constantly evolving all over the country as more and more African-Americans find meaning and inspiration in its rituals. You should feel free to invent your own traditions, songs, stories, rituals, and ways of celebrating. The list of "ingredients" for celebrating Kwanzaa (below) incorporates the symbols that form the backbone of the holiday. An excellent source for these items is your local black bookstore, which will either stock them, help you order them, or show you pictures of them so that you can make your own at home. The *karamu* feast (see pages 5–14) is also the occasion for the giving of creative *zawadi* gifts, although the gifts are not opened until the next day (see Chapter 7 for ideas and recipes for *zawadi* gifts from the kitchen). Chapter 5, "Cooking for Company," is a collection of recipes that can easily be adapted to feed as many guests as your house or hall can hold. In making gifts, cooking the feast, and assembling your Kwanzaa table, remember that uniting the African-American family and community is what Kwanzaa is about.

INGREDIENTS FOR CELEBRATING KWANZAA
1 black, red, and green *bendera ya taifa* flag
1 poster of the *nguzo saba*, the seven principles
1 straw mat *(mkeka)*
1 black candle
3 red candles
3 green candles
1 candle holder *(kinara)*
1 bowl of fruit and vegetables *(mazao)*
2 or more ears of corn *(muhindi)*
1 cup or goblet *(kikombe cha umoja,* or unity cup)
African art and sculptures, and books by and about
    Africans and African-Americans

The symbols used throughout the Kwanzaa celebration represent the ideas behind the holiday. For example, the *bendera ya taifa* flag is based on the black, red, and green striped one created by Marcus Garvey, founder of the nationalist movement. Black represents the people, red is for the struggle and the blood that has been shed, and green is for Africa and for the future. The *nguzo saba,* or seven principles, are posted as a constant reminder of the principles on which Kwanzaa is based.

Several items are displayed on a table throughout Kwanzaa. A straw mat, called a *mkeka,* is an essential item. The *mkeka* is a symbol of our history, the foundation of our culture. There is an African proverb that says: "No matter how high a house is built, it must stand on something." All the items used during the Kwanzaa celebration are placed on the *mkeka* to represent the past on which the present and the future are built.

One black, three red, and three green candles, called the *mishumaa saba,* are placed in a candle holder called a *kinara.* Each candle stands for one of the seven principles of Kwanzaa. The black candle is placed in the center and represents *umoja* (unity). It is lit during the first day of the celebration. The other candles are lit, one each day, from left to right. The green candles are placed on the left. They represent self-determination, collective work and responsibility, and cooperative economics *(kujichagulia, ujima,* and *ujamaa* in Swahili). The three red candles represent purpose, creativity, and faith *(nia, kuumba,* and *imani* in Swahili).

Mazao (a bowl of fruit and vegetables) and two or more ears of corn *(muhindi)* are placed on the *mkeka.* The fruit and vegetables represent the harvest, which is our reward for working together throughout the year. The ears of corn represent children, male and female, the future of the African-American community. Usually, an ear of corn is placed on the *mkeka* for each child who lives in the home. If there are no children in the home, two ears of corn are still placed on the table to illustrate the African belief that "it takes a whole village to raise a child."

The unity cup *(kikombe cha umoja)* is then placed on the *mkeka*. This cup is filled with water, wine, or grape juice at the *karamu* feast, which is held on December 31 (see pages 5–14). The cup is passed around after the libation statement. The libation statement is a way of remembering and honoring our ancestors, and also a heartfelt request for peace, prosperity, and harmony for the new year. The last items on the *mkeka* are African art and sculptures, and books by and about Africans and African-Americans.

To reinforce the principles of the *nguzo saba* each day, *"Habari gani?"* or "What's the news?" is the traditional morning greeting during the Kwanzaa holiday. The first day, the first principle *(umoja)* and its definition are the reply. Each day following, a new principle from the *nguzo saba* is used as a response.

The candle-lighting ceremony each evening gives you a chance to gather with friends and family and discuss the meaning of Kwanzaa. The first night, the black candle in the center is lit. Then the principle of unity *(umoja)* is discussed. One candle is lit each evening from left to right on each of the remaining days of the celebration and the appropriate principle discussed. You'll find ideas to start off your discussion in the following pages, in the introductions to each chapter. After the candle for the day has been lit, and the discussion is over, everyone shouts *"Harambee!"*—"Let's all pull together." *"Haram-*

bee" is shouted once on the first day of Kwanzaa. As each day passes, the number of times the saying is shouted increases by one. *"Harambee"* is said seven times on the seventh day of the celebration, January 1.

Many adults fast from sunup to sunset as a part of Kwanzaa. The fasting purifies the body and focuses the mind on the principle of the day. The evening meal is the only meal eaten. Afterwards, the candle-lighting ceremony is held.

In many areas, a community-wide Kwanzaa celebration is held on each night of the holiday. Some families join the community celebration after their candle-lighting ceremony is finished at home.

The Karamu Feast

On the sixth day of Kwanzaa, December 31, the Kwanzaa *karamu* feast is held. The *karamu* feast gathers together family and friends to celebrate our culture, our ancestors, and the community. This is also the event that brings together all the principles and ideas that Kwanzaa represents. The program below includes many rituals, any or all of which can be included in your Kwanzaa ceremony. One of the goals of the *karamu* feast is to give everyone a chance to express his or her feelings about Kwanzaa and the *nguzo saba* (seven principles). That's why there are so many opportunities to "testify." For example, seven guests can speak in the *kukumbuka* (reflections on the *nguzo saba*). But what if you have twenty? Well, there are as many other opportunities for expression as you want to include. You can read one libation statement, or three. You can have two cultural expressions, or five. Each guest should participate to the extent that he or she wishes, doing what he or she does best. Children should be encouraged to participate in every aspect of the Kwanzaa celebration. There are many recipes in this book which are easy enough for a child to prepare.

In the introductions to the chapters that follow, I've included my thoughts on what each *nguzo saba* principle means to me. If you're having trouble getting started, you could read them aloud, or just use them as starting points for your own discussion. All your guests should feel free to find their own way to express what the African-American heritage and community mean to them.

A typical program for a *karamu* feast is as follows:

Kukaribisha (Welcome)
Introductory Remarks and Recognition of Guests
and Elders
Cultural Expression
Kukumbuka (Remembrance and Reflections on
Kwanzaa)
Cultural Expression
Kuchunguza Tena Na Kutoa Ahadi Tena
(Reassessment and Recommitment)
Guest Speaker
Kushangilia (Rejoicing)
Tamshi la Tambiko (Libation Statement)
Kikombe cha Umoja (Passing of the Unity Cup)

Kutoa Majina (Calling the Names of Ancestors
and Heroes)
Ngoma (Drums)
Karamu (Feast)
Cultural Expression
Tamshi la Tutaonana (The Farewell Statement)

Many African-Americans wear African-style clothing
during the Kwanzaa celebration and the *karamu* feast.
The planning of the feast should be a cooperative effort,
and I've supplied a menu and recipes to assist you with
organizing the *karamu* meal. Serving the feast African
style, with pillows or cushions arranged around low ta-
bles, adds a festive and historic touch to the meal.

The color scheme for a *karamu* feast is black, red, and
green. The *kinara* and *mkeka* are an important part of
the celebration and are used during the *karamu*
ceremony.

The *karamu* celebration begins with a welcoming
speech called the *kukaribisha*, which is usually given by
one of the elders. Special guests and all the other elders
are recognized at this time.

Next, if you wish, give your guests a chance to express
what a principle of the *nguzo saba* means to them. One
by one, the guests light a candle and speak about the
principle the candle represents. This is called the *kukumbuka*.

After the candle-lighting ceremony is the time for cultural expression. This part of the ceremony features stories, songs, dances, skits, and other performances, and

occurs throughout the *karamu* program. It presents a great opportunity to get children excited about Kwanzaa. The *karamu* program can be as long or short as you wish.

Next, the *kuchunguza tena na kutoa ahadi tena* begins. This is the time for the guests to recommit themselves for the next year to the principles learned during Kwanzaa. Sometimes a guest speaker gives a speech on this topic. Then the *kushangilia,* or rejoicing, begins. Group songs are an inspiring way of rejoicing.

After the songs, the *tamshi la tambiko* (libation statement) is recited. This statement is like a prayer for the past, present, and future of the African-American community. The libation statement is the only part of the *karamu* feast that has a set text associated with it. That's because libation statements are used in some African harvest ceremonies. This is an Ashanti prayer:

> *The edges of the year have met*
> *I pray for life for the people*
> *May the nation prosper*
> *May the children be many*
> *May food come forth in abundance*
> *May no illness come*
> *May the people grow*
> *to be old men and women*
> *May no misfortune fall upon the land*
> *and for anyone who wishes evil on the people*
> *may misfortune fall on his own head.*

This is a Yoruba prayer:

O Creator, You who are the source of all wealth,
may we prosper.
You who turn blood into children,
make our children many.
Let us always wake in our own houses.
May our nations prosper
and our harvest always be abundant.

This is a modern libation statement:

For the Motherland cradle of civilization.
For the ancestors and their indomitable spirit.
For the elders from whom we can learn much.
For our youth who represent the promise for
  tomorrow.
For our people the original people.
For our struggle and in remembrance of those
who have struggled on our behalf.
For Umoja the principle of unity
which should guide us in all that we do.
For the Creator who provides all things great and
  small.

This is one I've composed:

We are not dwelling on the past, but we honor our
history, Africa, our ancient homeland, and our
ancestors,

*We are not frozen in the present, but we commit
ourselves to working toward the greatest good for
our people, our community, and our nation,*

*We cannot predict the future, but we are
optimistic, we are hopeful, and we are diligent in
our pursuit of success. We believe in our own
potential and abilities and in the potential and
abilities of our brothers and sisters to make the
dreams our ancestors had for us a reality,*

*We dedicate ourselves to be our brothers' and
sisters' keeper. We dedicate ourselves to watch over
our children. And we dedicate ourselves to the
principles of the* nguzo saba *now and throughout
the coming year.*

After the libation statement has ended, the unity cup
is filled with water, wine, or grape juice, and passed
around to everyone. The guests pretend to drink and a
small amount of the liquid is poured on the floor to honor
those who have died.

Next, the *kutoa majina,* or calling of the names of
family ancestors and African-American heroes, begins.
The names of deceased relatives and African-American
heroes and heroines are called out as a way of remembering them. When the last name has been called, the
ngoma, or drum, sounds. A drummer plays African-style
rhythms or a recording of African drum songs is played.
This is a signal for the start of the *karamu* feast.

Depending on where the feast is being held, the food
can be prepared cooperatively or each person may bring

a dish. The "Cooking for Company" chapter provides recipes that can be prepared in large quantities.

After the feast, singing, dancing, stories, and other forms of cultural expression continue, sometimes until midnight.

When the *karamu* celebration ends, the *tamshi la tutaonana* (farewell statement) is made. This contains your aspirations for the African-American community during the coming year and for the future. Each guest may participate or one person may speak for the group. At the end of the farewell statement, everyone shouts *Harambee!,* bringing the Kwanzaa *karamu* feast to an end.

Imani is the seventh and last day of Kwanzaa, and the first day of the new year. *Zawadi* gifts (see Chapter 7) can now be opened. The last day of Kwanzaa, *imani,* is devoted to faith, and the day should be used as a time of reflection over the principles and meaning of the *nguzo saba.* Hopefully, the principles and meaning of Kwanzaa will be practiced and fulfilled in your life and in the lives of your brothers and sisters throughout the rest of the year.

The Karamu Feast

In my family, good food is a sign of love. My interest in the art and technique of cooking is part of my heritage, a direct tie to my African ancestors.

Kwanzaa is an excellent time to recognize the many agricultural products and recipes that African and African-American cooks have contributed to America. African culinary techniques and the fruits, grains, and vegetables that were transported from Africa are a large part of our American diet. African cooking includes many creative uses for peppers, such as the *melegueta,* and spices, like ginger. Because African slaves did the majority of the cooking in many early American households, their influences are easy to detect. Credit for their creativity, however, is rarely given.

We relish spicy okra gumbos, sesame-covered snacks, expertly seasoned greens, dried and smoked fish, helpings of black-eyed peas and rice (Hoppin' John), and handfuls of peanuts without ever really considering how these foods came to America. African culinary techniques—from the preparation of stews and the uses of pepper sauces to the marinating and grilling of meats and vegetables—have been widely adopted, but not always credited to the culinary genius of African chefs.

Many African words, such as *gombo* (okra), *benne* (sesame seeds), *yams* (sweet potatoes), and *goobers* (ground peanuts), are still used today. The African captives knew how to make these native plants grow, and how to cook and season the dishes produced from them. Rice grows today in America mainly because African captives knew how to cultivate the plants.

Choosing recipes that contain ingredients which can be traced back to Africa is a culinary way of celebrating the principles of Kwanzaa. The recipes listed above contain many of the ingredients that African chefs used, and you may want to include them as part of your *karamu* feast.

1

Drinks, Appetizers, and Salads

UMOJA
(Unity)
To strive for and maintain unity in the family, community, nation, and the world African community.

When I think about my people, I see African-Americans of all colors and sizes standing shoulder to shoulder, hand in hand in a long line that reaches across mountains and valleys, rivers and oceans, all the way to Africa. We African-Americans are a people unified through blood, heredity, culture, and traditions. Although much of our ancient African history has been lost forever, we have forged a new history in America. Our ancestors may have been from different African tribes, but we have joined together in this new world to form one proud tribe.

We often hear about all the troubles that are tearing us apart as a people, but seldom about what holds us together. We instinctively root for one another, because we know the obstacles our brothers and sisters must overcome in order to succeed. We are our brothers' and sisters' keepers. Bad news may sell papers, but the good news is that through all the hardships, perils, and deprivations we've suffered we still rise, we still excel, we still go onward, and with a grace and a joy that are marvels to behold. Against all odds we are strong, we persevere.

Throughout our history in America we have united for a common cause. We helped one another during the terrible days when our ancestors first arrived in this country and were bought and sold like livestock. We relied on one another during the difficult early days of emancipation. We found homes, jobs, and food for one another during the great migration. We walked thousands of miles together to protest injustice during the civil rights movement. Today we protect one another, care for one another, vote for one another, and support one another. We are a mighty people. We have faced all manner of trials and we have triumphed.

The many acts of kindness that we do for one another will never be on the front page of a newspaper. Yet we all know that the spirit of unity our ancestors instilled in us lives on. We can see it in one another's eyes, we can see it in the eyes of our children. We know that our house may suffer cracks, but can never be divided no matter what forces work against it. For every negative word you hear about African-Americans, there are twenty things that are positive. We have pulled together in the past, we must pull together now, and we must pull together in the future. *Harambee!*

Spicy Mocha Punch

Yield: 12 8-ounce servings

The key to this punch is to use a strong, aromatic, high-quality coffee. Splurge a little! The flavor of this punch is well worth the price.

2 cups coffee
1½ sticks cinnamon, broken into halves
6 whole cloves
6 whole allspice
2 32-ounce cartons commercial eggnog
1 tablespoon vanilla extract
½ pint heavy cream, whipped
1 quart vanilla ice cream, softened
Ground nutmeg (optional)

In a small saucepan, combine the coffee, cinnamon, cloves, and allspice. Simmer for 15 minutes. Strain and discard the solids. Refrigerate the coffee mixture until chilled.

In a large mixing bowl, combine the coffee mixture with the eggnog and vanilla. Fold in the whipped cream. Place the mixture in a large punch bowl, and then add the softened ice cream. Sprinkle the punch with nutmeg.

Company Tea

Yield: 8 8-ounce servings

Tea is one of the most versatile and inexpensive drinks to prepare in large quantities. For a decorative touch, place mint leaves in the sections of an ice cube tray, cover them with water, and freeze. The frozen cubes of mint look very pretty in a glass or punch bowl.

3 quarts cold water
8 1-serving tea bags or 2 family-sized tea bags
½ cup sugar
2 6-ounce cans frozen lemonade
4 cups ginger ale
Mint leaves (optional)

In a medium saucepan, bring the water to a rolling boil. Place the tea bags in a heat-proof container. Pour the boiling water over the bags, cover the container, and let the tea steep for 5–10 minutes. Remove the tea bags and let the tea stand until cool. Mix in the sugar and lemonade and stir until the lemonade and sugar melt. Refrigerate. Stir in the gingerale just before serving. Garnish with frozen cubes of mint.

first fruits Punch

Yield: 14 8-ounce servings

"Before a group can enter the open society, it must first close ranks."

—STOKELY CARMICHAEL (KWAME TURE),
POLITICAL ACTIVIST

3 very ripe bananas
6 cups pineapple-orange juice
1 28-ounce bottle mineral water, chilled
1 25-ounce bottle sparkling cider, chilled
2 cups assorted sliced fruits (strawberries, oranges, kiwi, pineapples, or grapes)

Peel the bananas. Remove and discard any clinging banana "threads." Place the bananas in a blender and purée. In a large punch bowl, mix the bananas with the remaining ingredients. Serve chilled.

Harvest Cocktail

Yield: 4 8-ounce servings

Use this recipe to jazz up commercially prepared vegetable juice for a refreshingly different nonalcoholic drink.

4 cups vegetable juice
4 tablespoons minced onion
4 tablespoons finely chopped parsley
4 tablespoons lemon juice
½ teaspoon hot sauce
½ teaspoon Worcestershire sauce
1½ teaspoons sugar
½ teaspoon salt
4 stalks celery (optional)

Mix all the ingredients except the celery thoroughly. Chill for at least 1 hour. Strain the juice before serving. Place a stalk of celery in each glass, if desired.

Festive Cranberry Punch

Yield: 12 8-ounce servings

The almond extract brings out the flavor in this simple to prepare, deliciously different punch.

4 cups cranberry juice
1 46-ounce can pineapple juice
1½ cups sugar
1 teaspoon almond extract
4 cups ginger ale

In a large container, combine the cranberry juice, pineapple juice, sugar, and almond extract. Chill. Immediately before serving, stir in the gingerale. Serve over ice.

Winter Cider Punch

Yield: 12 8-ounce servings

This hot apple-flavored punch will fill your home with a delicious smell, giving a warm welcome to your Kwanzaa guests.

1 cup water
½ tablespoon ground ginger
½ tablespoon ground nutmeg
3 whole cloves
3 whole allspice
1 2-inch stick cinnamon
½ gallon apple cider
1½ cups sugar
¾ cup firmly packed light brown sugar

In a large saucepan, combine the water, ginger, nutmeg, cloves, allspice, and cinnamon. Cover and boil for 10 minutes. Reduce the heat to medium. Stirring frequently, continue cooking about 10 minutes. Add the apple cider and sugars. Turn heat to low and, stirring frequently, simmer for 10 minutes. Serve hot.

Ethiopian Party Punch

Yield: 12 8-ounce servings

"Let your motto be resistance! Resistance! RESIS-
TANCE! No oppressed people have ever secured
their liberty without resistance."

—HENRY HIGHLAND GARNET, ABOLITIONIST

1 cup cherry juice
1 cup strawberry syrup
1 cup orange juice
1 cup lemon juice
1 cup pineapple juice
1 cup white grape juice
2½ quarts lemon-lime soda
2 lemons, thinly sliced

Mix all the ingredients but the lemons together. Chill
and serve over ice. Garnish with lemon slices.

Sesame-Cheese Spread

Yield: 2 cups

In many African cultures, sesame seeds mean good luck. The tiny seeds traveled to America, often hidden in the hair of the captives. Sesame seeds, sesame oil, and dishes containing sesame are a delicious contribution our African ancestors made to American cuisine.

2 cups shredded sharp cheddar cheese
2 3-ounce packages cream cheese, softened
¼ cup toasted sesame seeds (see page 129)
¼ cup milk
1 teaspoon soy sauce
½ teaspoon dried or ground thyme
½ teaspoon salt

Mix all the ingredients in a blender or food processor until smooth. Scoop the spread into a serving bowl, cover, and refrigerate for at least 4 hours. Remove from the refrigerator at least 1 hour before serving and let it stand at room temperature. Serve with crackers or toast.

Stuffed Mushrooms

Yield: 8 servings

"Education is the primary tool of emancipation and liberation for African-Americans in our fight for true equality in this country."

—EARL G. GRAVES, PUBLISHER

3 pounds large mushrooms, stems removed
2 tablespoons olive oil

STUFFING:
2 10-ounce packages frozen chopped turnip greens
1 medium onion, minced
1 clove garlic, mashed
1 tablespoon butter or margarine
½ cup fresh fine breadcrumbs
1 teaspoon salt
1 teaspoon black pepper
½ teaspoon ground nutmeg
⅛ teaspoon Dijon mustard
⅓ cup grated Parmesan cheese

Preheat the broiler. On a lightly greased baking sheet (or 2 of them), place the mushrooms cap side up. Brush the caps with the olive oil, then broil them for 2 minutes, checking carefully to prevent them from burning. Remove the mushrooms from the oven and set aside.

To prepare the stuffing, cook the frozen turnip greens in a saucepan according to package directions. Add the minced onion, garlic, butter or margarine, breadcrumbs, salt, pepper, nutmeg, and mustard to the cooked greens. Mix the ingredients together until well blended. Turn the mushrooms cap side down. Fill each cap with a little of the greens mixture. Sprinkle with the Parmesan cheese. Broil until brown, about 2–5 minutes.

Moi-Moi

Yield: 4 servings

Serving black-eyed peas is a wonderful way to combine our culinary history with our cultural history during Kwanzaa. *Moi-moi* is a West African dish, and it's just one of the many ways Africans prepare black-eyed peas. Traditionally, the ground black-eyed peas were soaked overnight to remove the "eyes" on the skin of the peas. The peas were then pounded into a paste and wrapped in banana leaves. But removing the skin robs the peas of important nutrients. This modern version is prepared with skins intact, and with small squares of aluminum foil in place of the banana leaves.

2 cups dried black-eyed peas
1 medium onion, coarsely chopped
1 egg
¼ cup water
2 teaspoons chili powder
1 teaspoon salt
8 4-inch squares aluminum foil
Salsa for serving

Place the black-eyed peas in a medium bowl, cover them with water, and soak the peas overnight. Drain off the water. Place the peas, onion, egg, water, chili powder, and salt into the bowl of a food processor or blender.

Process until the ingredients form a smooth paste. Place 2 heaping tablespoons of the pea mixture on a square of aluminum foil. Tightly fold the foil around the mixture. Place the foil packets in a medium pot and cover them with water. Boil for 1 hour, until the *moi-moi* is firm. Serve hot or warm with spicy salsa.

Peanuts Piri-Piri

Yield: 8 servings

It is hard to determine exactly where the name *piri-piri*, or *pili-pili*, as it is known in some parts of Africa, originated. Some say it is a Portuguese word for the small red *melegueta* pepper. Others say it is a West African name for a small red peppercorn common to that region. In Mozambique, *piri-piri* is practically the national dish; the word refers to the spicy sauce used to coat nuts, beans, or plantains.

2 tablespoons vegetable oil
1 clove garlic, mashed
1 teaspoon chili powder
1 pound roasted shelled peanuts, unsalted
2 tablespoons lemon juice
½ teaspoon salt

Heat the oil in a medium skillet. Add the garlic and chili powder to the pan. Turn heat down to medium, and, stirring constantly, cook the ingredients for 2 minutes. Add the peanuts, lemon juice, and salt to the pan. Stir until the nuts are well coated. Serve warm.

Eggs Stuffed with Shrimp
(Ovos Recheados com Camarao)

Yield: 12 servings

Many African captives were taken to Brazil and sold as slaves, where they infused traditional Brazilian cuisine with their own recipes and cooking techniques. Now, the unique Afro-Brazilian cuisine is famous all over the world. This appetizer is a great twist on the traditional method of preparing deviled eggs.

12 eggs, hard-cooked and peeled
2 tablespoons butter
1 tablespoon minced onion
1 tablespoon chopped parsley
1 medium tomato, diced
½ cup cooked shrimp, minced
½ teaspoon garlic salt
½ teaspoon salt
½ teaspoon black pepper
1 egg, lightly beaten
1 tablespoon all-purpose flour
2 cups fresh breadcrumbs

Preheat the oven to 375 degrees. Slice the eggs in half lengthwise, as you would for deviled eggs. Remove the yolks and place them in a small bowl. Set the egg white halves aside. Mash the yolks with a fork until broken into small pieces; set aside. In a medium saucepan, melt the

✿ Boiling Eggs

Carefully place eggs in a large pot and set aside until they are at room temperature. Cover them with cold water to 1 inch above the tops. Bring the water to a boil. Reduce heat and simmer eggs for 15–20 minutes, gently stirring them every 2 or 3 minutes throughout the cooking time. If eggs are allowed to boil in one position, the yolks have a tendency to sink to the bottom of the egg. Stirring keeps the yolks in the center of the egg, which makes for more attractive presentation. Remove the eggs from the pot and run them under cool water. Crack the shells and run the eggs under cool water again. The eggs should peel easily.

butter. Sauté the onion, parsley, and tomato until the vegetables are wilted, about 3 minutes. Stir in the yolks, shrimp, garlic salt, salt, and pepper. Fill half an egg white with the shrimp mixture. Cover it with the other half of the egg white to make 1 whole egg. Repeat with remaining eggs.

In a small bowl, mix the raw egg and the flour together to make a paste. Roll the stuffed eggs in the flour paste and then in the breadcrumbs until all the eggs are coated. Place the eggs in a large, buttered baking dish. Bake until eggs are lightly browned, about 5–10 minutes.

Cheesy Black-eyed Pea Dip

Yield: 8 servings

"The study of economic oppression led me to realize that Negroes were not alone, but were part of an unending struggle for human dignity the world over."

—PAULI MURRAY, AUTHOR

1 stick butter or margarine
½ medium onion, chopped
2 5-ounce jars sharp pasteurized processed cheese or 8 ounces sharp cheddar
2 15-ounce cans black-eyed peas, drained
1 jalapeño pepper, seeds and ribs removed, diced
1 4-ounce can or 2 small fresh green chilies, chopped
½ teaspoon garlic salt

In a medium saucepan, melt the butter or margarine. Add the onion and sauté until golden brown. Turn heat to low, add the cheese, and stir until melted. Add the black-eyed peas, jalapeño, green chilies, and garlic salt. Cook for 5 minutes, stirring constantly. Serve hot.

✿ Preparing Hot Peppers

Remember to always wear gloves when preparing fresh hot peppers. If you don't, you'll experience a painful burning sensation in your hands and any other part of your body you touch. Never use hot water to rinse dried or fresh peppers, since it may cause fumes to rise, which will irritate your eyes and nose. Dried peppers may be crushed in a mortar and measured out in this form.

When preparing fresh hot peppers, it is best to remove the stems, ribs, and seeds with your gloved fingers. A paring knife may be used, however, if the ribs of the pepper are thick and fleshy. Removing the seeds from the peppers retains the flavor but greatly decreases the "heat." Always wash your hands thoroughly with soap and cold water when you are finished preparing the peppers. Be sure to clean any utensils or surfaces that have come in contact with the peppers.

Plantain Chips

Yield: 4 servings

"It is not so much a Negro History Week as it is History Week. We should emphasize not Negro History, but the Negro in history. What we need is not a history of selected races or nations, but the history of the world void of national bias, race hate, and religious prejudice."

—CARTER G. WOODSON, HISTORIAN

4 green or half-ripe plantains
2 teaspoons salt
Oil for frying

Peel the plantains and discard the skins. Cut the plantains at an angle into thin slices. Fill a medium bowl with cold water. Add 1 teaspoon of the salt and the plantain slices. Refrigerate for 30 minutes.

In a large skillet, heat 2 inches of oil. Drain the plantain slices and dry them on paper towels. Place a quarter of the plantains in the oil and fry them until the slices are light brown, about 3–5 minutes. Place the fried plantain on paper towels to drain. Repeat with the other slices. Sprinkle the plantain chips with salt and serve warm.

Date and Peanut Salad

Yield: 8 servings

"The basic tenet of black consciousness is that the black man must reject all value systems that seek to make him a foreigner in the country of his birth and reduce his basic human dignity."

—STEVE BIKO, ACTIVIST

2 cups dates, pitted and chopped
½ cup peanuts, chopped
2 cups minced celery
1 cup French salad dressing

In a medium salad bowl, mix all the ingredients until well blended. Refrigerate until time to serve.

Ham and Black-eyed Pea Salad

Yield: 6 servings

This is a great salad to serve for a New Year's Day lunch party, and a delicious way to make sure you've had your quota of black-eyed peas so your luck will hold for another 364 days!

3 15-ounce cans black-eyed peas
2 cups cubed cooked ham
1 cup chopped celery
1 large green bell pepper, ribs and seeds removed, chopped
1 medium onion, chopped
1 teaspoon yellow mustard
1 cup mayonnaise, or to taste
1 teaspoon salt
1 teaspoon black pepper

Drain the black-eyed peas and place them in a large bowl. Stir in the remaining ingredients and mix well. Refrigerate.

Okra Salad
(Salada de Quiabo)

Yield: 6 servings

When I was younger, just the thought of eating okra made me cringe. Like many people, I thought of okra as a limp, slimy vegetable. But when properly prepared, okra has a wonderful taste. Its texture is perfect for this salad, which is popular in Brazil.

1 10-ounce package frozen whole okra
1 tablespoon lemon juice
1 tablespoon chopped onion
½ teaspoon black pepper
½ cup French dressing, or to taste
½ pound salad greens (shredded cabbage, endive,
    watercress, romaine, spinach, or iceberg lettuce)
2 hard-cooked eggs (see page 31), sliced into rounds
6 whole black olives

Cook okra according to the package directions. Drain and cool. Place the okra in a medium bowl and sprinkle with the lemon juice. Add the onion, pepper, and French dressing. Toss gently until the okra is well coated. Divide the salad greens on 6 small plates. Arrange the okra on top of the greens. Add a few slices of the egg. Place an olive in the center of each plate.

Cornbread Salad

Yield: 10 servings

This salad is so unusual that when I heard about it, I had to try it. After I tried it, I had to include it. As our enslaved ancestors knew, with a little ingenuity, just about anything can be turned into a wonderful meal.

4 cups cooked cornbread (about 1 13 × 9 × 2-inch pan), crumbled
2 cups mayonnaise, or to taste
2 stalks celery, chopped
1 large green bell pepper, ribs and seeds removed, chopped
1 4-ounce jar chopped pimientos
¾ cup chopped green onion
¾ cup chopped pecans
2 large tomatoes, diced
10 lettuce leaves

In a large bowl, combine all the ingredients but the lettuce until well blended. Place the salad in the refrigerator until thoroughly chilled. Serve individual salad portions mounded on a lettuce leaf.

Jambalaya Salad

Yield: 8 servings

"I thought that this beautiful feeling I'd shared with my immediate family was exclusive to them. I saw instead that the black feelings—the warmth, the love, the laughter, the spontaneity—extended beyond my household. It was as though my own family had just grown larger."

—JANET JACKSON, SINGER

1 cup mayonnaise, or to taste
2 tablespoons yellow mustard
3 tablespoons French dressing
1 clove garlic, mashed
2 cups cooked rice, cooled
1 cup diced celery
2½ cups diced tomatoes
½ cup chopped green bell pepper, ribs and seeds removed

In a medium bowl, combine the mayonnaise, mustard, French dressing, and garlic. Add the rice, celery, tomatoes, and bell pepper. Toss until well blended. Refrigerate.

Black Bean Salad

Yield: 16 servings

"I have the people behind me and the people are
my strength."

—HUEY P. NEWTON,
A FOUNDER OF THE BLACK PANTHER PARTY

4 16-ounce cans black beans
1 large purple onion, minced
1 large red bell pepper, ribs and seeds removed,
   minced
1 large green bell pepper, ribs and seeds removed,
   minced
1 bunch parsley, stems removed, chopped
3 tablespoons chopped cilantro
3 teaspoons ground cumin
1 teaspoon salt
1 teaspoon black pepper
1 tablespoon lemon juice
½ cup olive oil
½ teaspoon hot sauce

Drain the black beans and place them in a large bowl.
Add the rest of the ingredients and toss until well
blended. Refrigerate the salad until 1 hour before serving; it should be at room temperature.

Chicken and Spinach Salad

Yield: 4 servings

"In all things that are purely social we can be separate as the fingers, yet one as the hand in all things essential to mutual progress."

—BOOKER T. WASHINGTON, EDUCATOR

4 slices bacon
¼ cup white vinegar
2 teaspoons sugar
1 teaspoon cornstarch
½ teaspoon salt
¼ teaspoon black pepper
2 cups cubed cooked chicken
1 tablespoon sesame seeds
1 pound fresh spinach, washed thoroughly to remove grit
½ small purple onion, thinly sliced

In a large pot, fry the bacon until crisp. Remove bacon slices to a paper towel-covered plate to drain, but reserve the bacon fat in the pot. Crumble the bacon slices and set aside. Add the vinegar, sugar, cornstarch, salt, and pepper to the pot. Heat to boiling, stirring constantly. Stir in the chicken and sesame seeds. Cook for another minute. Remove the pot from the heat.

Add the spinach and onion; toss until the spinach is wilted, about 2–3 minutes. Sprinkle with the chopped bacon and serve immediately.

✤ Cleaning Spinach

Spinach has a lovely, fresh flavor. But it also has a tendency to retain large amounts of sand and dirt. Improperly cleaned spinach will ruin a recipe.

When shopping for spinach, look for tender, bright-green unblemished leaves. Remove and discard any leaves that are discolored as well as the roots. Let gravity work for you by allowing the spinach to stay in a basin full of cool water for several minutes. Most of the dirt will sink to the bottom of the basin. Remove the spinach, and drain and rinse the basin. Repeat this washing process several times to remove all the grit.

2

Soups and Stews

KUJICHAGULIA
(Self-determination)
To define ourselves, name ourselves, create for ourselves,
and speak for ourselves instead of being defined, named,
created for, and spoken for by others.

All of us, regardless of race or gender, undertake the life
task of finding out who we are. We all ask ourselves
questions about what we truly think and feel. We all
struggle with being faithful to our feelings and how we
have defined ourselves. We African-Americans have a
more difficult journey on the road to finding ourselves
because so much of our past has been stolen from us.
One's past shapes one's future. As an African-American
woman and writer, I have spent a lot of time and energy
reconstructing my past so that I can see my future
clearly.

It has been a long, hard journey along the road to self-
discovery, but I have reached the point where I can say I

am comfortable with my skin and in my skin. I am admiring but not envious of others, because I love being myself. I would rather laugh than cry, so I look for the humorous part of unpleasant situations. I know who I am, and I embrace the best parts of myself without succumbing to despair about the worse parts. I know that there is some good in every situation, no matter how bad it may look. I have finally found the patience to search for that tiny glimmer of goodness.

In my quest to find myself, I've often examined the lives of African-Americans in the past and in my own personal history. My grandparents on both sides were all remarkable people. They have such a strong presence that although they've been dead for many years, the force of their personalities lives on in my daily life. The stories I have heard about them have helped to shape the person I've become today. My parents are two of the most determined people I know. They've knocked down, walked around, squeezed under, and broken through the barriers of poverty, racism, and sexism because when they set a goal for themselves, no one is going to stop them. My father's perseverance in his personal and professional life has had a positive impact on my life. My mother astounded us all when, after thirty years of being a homemaker, she decided to go to college to become an interior decorator. She attended classes with students young enough to be her own children. Now she has had a successful career for more than twenty years. It was something she had always wanted to do and she did it.

I have drawn strength during the long road I've traveled to find out who I am from many other determined African-American men and women. I've always felt a strong kinship with Ida B. Wells-Barnett. She was an amazing woman. Her courage and stamina have been a constant inspiration to me as a woman and as a writer. After losing both parents and her baby brother during a yellow fever epidemic in Holly Springs, Mississippi, in 1876, Ida became the head of her family at age fourteen. She was determined to keep her three sisters and two brothers together as a family. She lengthened her skirts, left childhood behind, and took a job that paid $25 a month as a teacher at a rural school.

Ida never let her race, her sex, or her height (she was a tiny woman) stand in the way of her dreams. She fought against discrimination in court after she was asked to take a seat in the segregated car of a train; in print as a journalist and as owner of the *Memphis Free Speech;* and in person as one of the foremost investigators of lynchings in the South. To me, her life is an example of the power of the printed word. She proved that the pen is mightier than the sword with her scathing articles on racism. She organized the women she knew into a political force and became a model for African-American women's clubs around the United States. She also founded the Negro Fellowship League, an organization that helped African-Americans with housing and job assistance. Ida had a wonderful career, and her union with attorney Ferdinand Lee Barnett was an example of a loving, strong, supportive marriage. Together they had four children. For Ida nothing was seen as a hindrance. She knew that when you have a goal in mind, and many things to juggle, you have the ability to grow an extra pair of hands in order to get the job done.

Ida B. Wells-Barnett is only one example of an African-American speaking, defining, creating, and determining his or her life. On the road to self-determination the pitfalls, roadblocks, and detours may slow you down, but you must always continue the journey toward self-discovery. As in every journey, you will reach a resting place where you can think about where you are, look back and see where you've come from, and look forward and see where you have to go. The qualities you learn about yourself along the road are what make the journey worthwhile.

Chickpea and Sausage Soup

Yield: 6 servings

"Self-help is the best help."

—AESOP, PHILOSOPHER

1 pound spicy Italian sausage, removed from casings
1 medium onion, chopped
3 cups water
½ teaspoon dried or ground basil
½ teaspoon dried or ground oregano
2 carrots, sliced
1 medium zucchini, halved and sliced
1 10¾-ounce can condensed tomato soup
1 15-ounce can stewed tomatoes, with liquid
1 can chickpeas (garbanzo beans), drained
¼ teaspoon ground red pepper (cayenne)
1 teaspoon salt
¼ cup grated Parmesan cheese

In a large pot or 4-quart Dutch oven, cook the sausage and onion over medium heat until the sausage is light brown and the onions wilted. Drain off the fat. Stir in all of the remaining ingredients except the Parmesan cheese. Heat to boiling, stirring constantly. Reduce the heat, cover, and simmer for 20 minutes, or until the vegetables are tender. Serve sprinkled with Parmesan cheese.

Easy Peanut Soup

Yield: 10 servings

"It's not what you call us, but what we answer to that matters."

—DJUKA, PHILOSOPHER

1 stick butter or margarine
1 medium onion, minced
1 cup sliced celery
2 tablespoons all-purpose flour
4 14½-ounce cans chicken broth
1 cup creamy peanut butter
1 cup half-and-half
¼ teaspoon ground red pepper (cayenne)
1 teaspoon salt
¼ cup chopped salted peanuts and/or ¼ cup chopped green onions, for garnish (optional)

Melt the butter or margarine in a large pot over medium-low heat. Sauté the onion and celery until the onion has wilted and the celery is tender. Mix in the flour, stirring until well blended. Slowly add the chicken broth, stirring frequently, and cook until the mixture comes to a boil. Immediately reduce the heat to a simmer. Remove 1 cup of the broth, mix it with the peanut butter, half-and-half, red pepper, and salt in a small bowl, then stir this mixture into the remaining broth. Simmer for 10 minutes, stirring frequently. Garnish with chopped peanuts or green onions.

Celebration Soup

Yield: 10 servings

"It is far better to be free to govern, or misgovern, yourself than to be governed by anybody else."

—KWAME NKRUMAH, FORMER PRESIDENT OF GHANA

½ stick butter
2 medium onions, chopped
3 stalks celery, chopped
2 tablespoons all-purpose flour
1 tablespoon curry powder
1 cup diced cooked chicken
2 apples, peeled, cored, and chopped
8 cups chicken broth
1 bay leaf
1 cup light cream, chilled

In a large saucepan, melt the butter over medium heat. Add the onions and celery. Sauté the vegetables until the onions are golden brown and the celery is soft. Stir in the flour and curry powder. Cook for 5 minutes. Place the mixture in a blender or food processor. Add the chicken, apples, and 1 cup of the chicken broth. Process until smooth. Return the mixture to the saucepan. Add the remaining 7 cups chicken broth and the bay leaf. Increase the heat to high to bring ingredients to a boil. When the soup begins to boil, remove it from the heat, discard the bay leaf, and refrigerate the soup at least 1 hour. Before serving, stir in the chilled cream.

Sweet Potato Soup

Yield: 6 servings

"We wanted something for ourselves and for our children, so we took a chance with our lives."

—UNITA BLACKWELL,
POLITICIAN AND CIVIL RIGHTS ACTIVIST

2 medium sweet potatoes
3 tablespoons butter
1 medium onion, minced
4 14½-ounce cans beef broth
3 medium tomatoes, finely chopped
1 teaspoon salt
1 teaspoon black pepper
½ teaspoon ground ginger
1 cup milk

In a large pot of water, boil the sweet potatoes until tender when pricked with a fork, about 30–35 minutes. Peel the potatoes when they're cool enough to handle, then mash them in a bowl with a potato masher or the back of a large spoon. Set aside.

Over medium heat, melt the butter in the pot. Add the onion and sauté until wilted. Add the beef broth, tomatoes, salt, pepper, and ginger. Cook until heated through, about 5 minutes. Add the mashed potatoes and milk. Simmer over low heat for 5 minutes, stirring until smooth and free of lumps.

Sparerib Stew

Yield: 8 servings

"If I didn't define myself for myself, I would be crunched into other people's fantasies for me and eaten alive."

—AUDRE LORDE, POET

1 tablespoon salt
1 tablespoon Worcestershire sauce
1 teaspoon ground cumin
½ teaspoon black pepper
½ teaspoon dried or ground oregano
2 bay leaves, crumbled
½ clove garlic, mashed
1 medium onion, chopped
1½ tablespoons cider vinegar
2½-pounds spareribs, cut into serving pieces
4 cups cold water
2 cups potatoes cut into 1-inch cubes
1 15-ounce can corn or 1 10-ounce package frozen corn
½ cup milk

In a large bowl, mix together the salt, Worcestershire sauce, cumin, pepper, oregano, bay leaves, garlic, onion, and vinegar. Add the spareribs to the bowl, coating the meat with the seasonings. Refrigerate for 8–10 hours or overnight. Place the ribs and any loose seasonings in a large pot. Add the water. Cover and simmer the meat over low heat for about 1 hour, or until tender.

Add the potatoes, corn, and milk. Cover and simmer until the potatoes are tender, about 10–15 minutes.

Seafood Gumbo

Yield: 6 servings

"I thought I could change the world. It took me a hundred years to figure out I can't change the world. I can only change Bessie. And honey, that ain't easy either."

—BESSIE DELANY, DOCTOR AND AUTHOR

½ stick butter or margarine
2 medium onions, sliced
1 medium green bell pepper, ribs and seeds removed, cut into strips
2 cloves garlic, mashed
2 tablespoons all-purpose flour
3 cups water
1 tablespoon instant beef bouillon granules
1 teaspoon salt
½ teaspoon black pepper
½ teaspoon hot sauce
1 bay leaf
1 10-ounce package frozen cut okra, thawed
1 16-ounce can whole tomatoes, with liquid, chopped
1 6-ounce can tomato paste
1½ pounds fresh or thawed frozen shrimp, shelled and deveined
1 pound cooked crabmeat
1 dozen oysters, with liquid
3 cups hot cooked rice, for serving

In a large pot or Dutch oven, melt the butter or margarine. Add the onions, bell pepper, and garlic. Sauté until the vegetables are tender, about 3 minutes. Reduce the heat to a simmer, add the flour, and, stirring constantly, cook until the mixture is bubbly, about 5–8 minutes. Add the water, bouillon, salt, pepper, hot sauce, bay leaf, okra, tomatoes, and tomato paste. Stir until well blended. Increase the heat to high and bring to a boil. Reduce the heat and simmer, uncovered, stirring occasionally, for 40 minutes. Add the shrimp, crabmeat, and oysters; cover the pot and cook another 5 minutes. Serve the gumbo over mounds of rice.

Trinidad Callalo Stew

Yield: 6 servings

"Can't nothin make your life work if you ain't the architect."

—TERRY McMILLAN, AUTHOR

1 pound fresh spinach or Swiss chard, washed and chopped
4 ounces lean salt pork, cut into ½-inch cubes
1 medium onion, diced
1 clove garlic, mashed
3 whole green onions, chopped
3 14½-ounce cans chicken broth
¼ teaspoon dried or ground thyme
1 teaspoon salt
1 teaspoon black pepper
½ pound fresh, canned, or frozen cooked crabmeat
½ cup canned coconut milk
½ pound fresh okra or 1 10-ounce package frozen whole okra, thawed and sliced
Hot sauce to taste

Place the greens in a large pot or Dutch oven. Add the salt pork, onion, garlic, green onions, chicken broth, thyme, salt, and pepper. Cover the pot and simmer over low heat, stirring occasionally, until the greens and salt pork are tender, about 20 minutes. Add the crabmeat, coconut milk, and okra. Cook until the okra is tender, about 10 minutes. Season to taste with hot sauce.

3

Main Dishes

UJIMA

(Collective Work and Responsibility)

To build and maintain our community together and to make our sisters' and brothers' problems our problems and to solve them together.

Marian Barnes, a writer and storyteller who lives in Austin, Texas, has written a wonderful creed that is a perfect illustration of *ujima*—collective work and responsibility:

> If no one will teach me,
> I will teach myself, and then
> I will teach someone else.
>
> If no one will help me,
> I will help myself, and then
> I will help someone else.
>
> If no one will save me,
> I will save myself, and then
> I will save somebody else.

> If no one will give me a job,
> I will make a job for myself, and then
> I will make a job for somebody else.

The African-American community faces many challenges. Often, it seems that there are more problems than there are solutions, more people in need than there are those to help. I've often felt overwhelmed by the adversity we face as a community. Lately, I've also come to the realization that I can't solve all the problems, but I can solve some of them. When I take the time to search for an answer to just one of the problems in my neighborhood, I know I'm making a significant contribution. A community is made up of a group of individuals. Individually, we can make a difference that will benefit our whole community. Together, we can conquer the world of problems we face as a race.

I enjoy working with and writing books for children. But in my travels, I often encounter children who have poor reading skills, to whom reading is more struggle than pleasure. In 1987, with my husband's help, I started a small organization called Book Boosters. I spent one hour a day, five days a week, tutoring small groups of children in area elementary schools. The first donation we received was fifty dollars. I spent the money on books, which we gave to the children. Now, Book Boosters is a fully funded nonprofit organization with a full-time salaried reading teacher and a staff of tutors. We've successfully tutored more than a thousand elementary school students. We provide them with the skills to read the new books they receive through the program. Through Book Boosters, I've learned that one person can make a difference in a community.

The late Clara McBride Hale (or Mother Hale, as she was often called) ran a day-care center for years. For a dollar extra, parents could leave their children at her house day AND night. She raised forty children this way, plus a son and daughter of her own. "Every one of them went to college, every one of them graduated, and they have lovely jobs. They're some of the nicest people," said Mother Hale.

In 1969, Mother Hale decided to retire. A few years later, her daughter, Dr. Lorraine Hale, encountered a young mother who was addicted to drugs. This woman needed someone who would care for her baby while she was in rehabilitation. The child was born addicted to the drugs in her mother's body. Dr. Hale asked her mother if she would care for the child. Mother Hale opened her arms and her heart. That is how Hale House began—in a Harlem brownstone, with a staff of one, in 1973.

"Inside of two months, I had twenty-two babies living in a five-room apartment," said Mother Hale. "My decision to stop didn't mean anything. It seems as though God wanted them. He kept sending them and He kept opening a way for me to make it. It's been over six hundred addicted babies. . . . It's back to being very bad for black people now. But I'll live through that, too. If I don't, I have a daughter that will carry on. I have grandchildren and great-grandchildren. They have the same feeling.

When I'm gone, somebody else will take it up and do it. This is how we've lived all these years."

It takes a decision by only one member of the community to make life better for all. That's how we've lived all these years.

Moroccan Honey Chicken

Yield: 8 servings

"Our elevation must be the result of self-efforts and work of our own hands. No other human power can accomplish it. If we but determine it shall be so, it will be so."

—MARTIN R. DELANEY, POLITICIAN AND AUTHOR

2 16-ounce cans stewed tomatoes, with liquid
1 large onion, chopped
4 cloves garlic, mashed
1 6-ounce can tomato paste
1½ teaspoons salt
¼ teaspoon black pepper
1 tablespoon plus 1 teaspoon ground cinnamon
2 teaspoons ground ginger
¼ cup plus 2 tablespoons honey
2 2- to 3-pound chickens, cut into serving pieces
2 tablespoons toasted sesame seeds (optional; see page 129)

In a large pot or Dutch oven, combine the tomatoes, onion, garlic, tomato paste, ½ teaspoon of the salt, the pepper, 1 tablespoon of the cinnamon, the ginger, and ¼ cup of the honey. Over low heat, mix the ingredients together until well blended. Add the chicken to the pot, spoon the sauce over the pieces, cover, and cook for 1 hour, or until the chicken is tender. Remove the chicken pieces from the pot and set aside. Boil the remaining sauce, stirring occasionally, until it thickens somewhat, about 10 minutes. Add the remaining 2 tablespoons honey, 1 teaspoon cinnamon, and 1 teaspoon salt to the sauce. Return the chicken to the pot and heat through, about 5–10 minutes. Serve the chicken covered with the sauce. Sprinkle with sesame seeds, if desired.

Oven-Fried Chicken with Herbs

Yield: 8 servings

"The economic philosophy of black nationalism only means that our people need to be re-educated in the importance of controlling the economy of the community in which we live."

—MALCOLM X

½ cup olive oil
1 stick butter or margarine, melted
4 cups all-purpose flour
1 tablespoon salt
2 teaspoons garlic powder
2 teaspoons dried or ground sage
2 teaspoons dried or ground marjoram
2 teaspoons dried or ground thyme
2 teaspoons black pepper
¼ teaspoon ground red pepper (cayenne)
2 2- to 3-pound chickens, cut into serving pieces

Preheat the oven to 375 degrees. In a large bowl, stir the olive oil and butter together. Place the flour, salt, garlic powder, sage, marjoram, thyme, black pepper, and red pepper in a large plastic bag or brown paper bag. Shake the ingredients to blend them. Coat 3 pieces of chicken in the olive oil–butter mixture, then drop them into the bag containing the seasoned flour. Shake until the chicken pieces are well coated. For crispier chicken, coat the flour-covered pieces in the oil again and then recoat the pieces with more flour. Place the chicken on a paper towel–covered plate and repeat the process until all the chicken pieces are coated. Refrigerate for 1 hour.

On a cookie sheet or in a shallow baking pan, place the chicken skin side up with space between pieces. Drizzle the chicken pieces with the remaining oil mixture. Bake for 45 minutes. Turn the pieces over and bake another 15 minutes, or until done.

Broiled Lemon Chicken

Yield: 4 servings

"A single bracelet does not jingle."

—CONGO PROVERB

1 2½- to 3-pound broiler-fryer, split in two
1 cup vegetable oil
¾ cup lemon juice
1 tablespoon garlic salt
1 tablespoon minced parsley
½ cup minced onion
2 teaspoons dried or ground basil
2 teaspoons dried or ground thyme
1 teaspoon black pepper

Place the chicken halves in a large bowl. Mix the remaining ingredients to form a marinade and pour it over the chicken. Marinate the chicken for several hours or overnight, turning occasionally.

Preheat the over broiler. Place the chicken halves skin side up in a shallow baking pan. Reserve the marinade for basting. Broil the chicken until brown, about 15–20 minutes, basting occasionally with the remaining marinade. Turn the chicken over and baste once with the marinade, then discard any unused marinade. Do NOT BASTE after this point. Broil another 15–20 minutes, until the chicken is brown and tender.

Sesame Crunch Chicken

Yield: 4 servings

"If there is no struggle, there is no progress."
—FREDERICK DOUGLASS,
STATESMAN, PUBLISHER, JOURNALIST

⅔ cup evaporated milk
2 tablespoons plus 1 teaspoon Worcestershire sauce
1 teaspoon salt
1 teaspoon garlic salt
⅛ teaspoon hot sauce
1 2½- to 3-pound chicken, cut into serving pieces
¾ cup crumbled cornflakes
¼ cup sesame seeds
2 tablespoons butter or margarine, melted

In a large bowl, combine the evaporated milk, 2 tablespoons of the Worcestershire sauce, the salt, garlic salt, and hot sauce. Mix well. Add the chicken, turning each piece to coat it. Cover tightly and refrigerate for 2 hours or longer.

Preheat the oven to 350 degrees. Combine the cornflake crumbs with the sesame seeds. Roll the chicken in the crumb mixture until well coated. Place the chicken skin side up in a shallow baking pan. Combine the melted butter or margarine with the remaining 1 teaspoon Worcestershire sauce. Drizzle this sauce over the chicken. Bake the chicken 1 hour, or until it is cooked through and the skin is crisp.

Karamu Chicken

Yield: 6 servings

"As long as we agree on objectives, we should never
fall out with each other just because we believe in
different methods or tactics or strategy. . . . We have
to keep in mind at all times that we are not fighting
for integration, nor are we fighting for separation.
We are fighting for recognition as free humans in
this society."

—MALCOLM X

1 2½- to 3-pound chicken, cut into serving pieces
⅓ cup plus ¼ cup French dressing
1 16-ounce can stewed tomatoes, with liquid, chopped
½ medium onion, sliced
2 stalks celery, chopped
1 teaspoon salt
1 teaspoon sweet paprika
½ teaspoon black pepper
¼ cup water
2 tablespoons all-purpose flour

In a large skillet over low heat, sauté the chicken pieces
in ⅓ cup of the French dressing until lightly browned.
Remove the chicken from the skillet. Add the tomatoes,
onion, celery, salt, paprika, pepper, and the remaining ¼
cup of the French dressing to the skillet. Stir until well
blended. Return the chicken pieces to the skillet, cover,

and simmer for 45 minutes, or until the chicken is done. Remove to a serving platter.

In a small bowl, gradually add the water to the flour. Stir until well blended and smooth. Pour the flour mixture into the pan juices, turn the heat to high, and bring the sauce to a boil. Lower the heat and cook, stirring constantly, until the sauce thickens. Pour the sauce over the chicken.

Spareribs with Sweet Potato Dressing

Yield: 6 servings

"A community is democratic only when the humblest and weakest person can enjoy the highest civil, economic, and social rights that the biggest and most powerful possess."

—A. PHILIP RANDOLPH,
FOUNDER OF THE BROTHERHOOD
OF SLEEPING CAR PORTERS

2 large slabs of spareribs, about 2 pounds each
2 tablespoons steak sauce
2 tablespoons Worcestershire sauce
2 teaspoons salt
2 teaspoons black pepper
2 teaspoons garlic powder
1 teaspoon dried or ground sage
½ cup all-purpose flour
Sweet Potato Dressing (recipe follows)
2 cups boiling water

Preheat the oven to 325 degrees. Rinse the spareribs and remove excess fat. Rub each slab on both sides with a tablespoon of the steak sauce and a tablespoon of the Worcestershire sauce. Mix the salt, pepper, garlic powder, sage, and flour together. Coat the slabs with the flour mixture. Spread the Sweet Potato Dressing on the concave part of each slab. Fold the slabs in half, securing the meat with a skewer if necessary. Place the slabs in a baking pan and pour in the boiling water. Bake, uncovered, for 1½–2 hours, until the meat is tender.

Sweet Potato Dressing

    2 cups cooked, mashed sweet potatoes
    1 cup cooked rice
    1½ cups minced celery
    2 tablespoons butter or margarine, melted
    1 tablespoon minced onion
    1 teaspoon salt
    1 teaspoon black pepper

Mix all the ingredients until well blended.

Pork Chops with Green Peppers

Yield: 6 servings

This is an easy dish to make for company.

½ cup all-purpose flour
1 teaspoon salt
1 teaspoon black pepper
6 lean loin or rib pork chops
2 tablespoons butter
2 cups Bloody Mary drink mix
1 large green bell pepper, ribs and seeds removed, sliced
into rings

Preheat the oven to 350 degrees. Put the flour, salt, and pepper in a plastic bag. Add the pork chops, a few at a time, and shake until the chops are well coated. Melt the butter in a medium skillet, then brown the chops on both sides, 2 at a time. In a shallow baking dish, place the pork chops close together. Pour the Bloody Mary mix over the chops and lay the bell pepper rings on top. Cover the baking dish with aluminum foil. Bake the pork chops about 30 minutes, or until done. Remove the foil and cook 15 minutes longer to brown the chops. Serve with the pan juices.

Spicy Short Ribs

Yield: 6 servings

"There are few things in the world as dangerous as sleepwalkers."

—RALPH ELLISON, AUTHOR

3 pounds beef short ribs, excess fat removed
1 teaspoon salt
¼ teaspoon black pepper
1 pound carrots, peeled and halved crosswise
1 pound baking potatoes, peeled and halved crosswise
1 15-ounce can green beans or 1 pound fresh green
  beans, trimmed and cut into 1-inch pieces
1 medium onion, chopped
1 15-ounce can beef broth
2 tablespoons horseradish
2 teaspoons mustard
2 tablespoons all-purpose flour
½ cup water

Preheat the oven to 350 degrees. Place the ribs in a large baking dish. Season with the salt and pepper. Bake, uncovered, for 2 hours. Drain and discard the fat. Place the carrots, potatoes, green beans, and onion around the ribs. In a small mixing bowl, stir together the broth, horseradish, and mustard. Pour the mixture over the meat, cover the pan with aluminum foil, and bake another 1–1½ hours, or until the meat is tender. To thicken the gravy, strain the pan juices into a saucepan. Return any vegetables to the baking pan. Skim off any fat from the pan juices. Mix the flour and water together until smooth, then add to the saucepan. Stirring constantly, bring the gravy to a boil over medium heat. Boil and stir for 1 minute. Serve gravy with ribs and vegetables.

Marinaded Beef Brisket

Yield: 10 servings

"No matter what accomplishment you make, somebody helps you."

—ALTHEA GIBSON, ATHLETE

1 8- to 10-pound brisket, excess fat removed
1 tablespoon garlic powder
½ tablespoon salt
½ tablespoon black pepper
1 teaspoon celery salt
¼ cup liquid smoke (optional)
4 tablespoons Worcestershire sauce
4 tablespoons steak sauce

Place the brisket in a large baking dish or Dutch oven. Rub the garlic powder, salt, pepper, celery salt, optional liquid smoke, Worcestershire sauce, and steak sauce all over the meat. Cover the baking dish tightly with a sheet of heavy-duty aluminum foil, and marinate the brisket overnight in the refrigerator. Bake, covered, for 7 hours at 225 degrees, or until done.

Cheese Steaks

Yield: 6 servings

"The struggle may be a moral one; or it may be a physical one; or it may be both moral and physical; but it must be a struggle. Power concedes nothing without a demand."

—FREDERICK DOUGLASS,
STATESMAN, PUBLISHER, JOURNALIST

¼ cup shortening
2 pounds round steak, cut into 1-inch strips
2 cups chopped onions
3 tablespoons all-purpose flour
1 16-ounce can whole tomatoes, with liquid
2 teaspoons salt
2 teaspoons chili powder
¼ teaspoon black pepper
4 ounces cheddar cheese, grated

Preheat the oven to 350 degrees. In a large skillet, melt the shortening and brown the steak strips on both sides. Place the steak pieces in a large baking dish. Put the onions in the skillet and sauté over medium heat until wilted. Add the flour and stir for about a minute. Add the tomatoes, salt, chili powder, and pepper. Cook for 3 minutes, stirring, to blend all the ingredients and break up the tomatoes. Pour the tomato mixture over the meat, cover, and bake for 2 hours. Remove the cover and sprinkle the meat with grated cheese. Bake uncovered for 3–5 minutes, or until the cheese melts.

Caribbean Curried Steak

Yield: 6 servings

"Strategy is better than strength."

—HAUSA PROVERB

4 tablespoons vegetable oil
1 clove garlic, mashed
1 small jalapeño pepper, ribs and seeds removed,
  finely chopped (see page 33)
2 green onions, chopped
2 medium onions, chopped
2 pounds sirloin steak, cut into 1-inch strips
1 tablespoon curry powder
1 teaspoon ground ginger
2 cups coconut milk or water

Heat the oil in a large skillet. Add the garlic, jalapeño, green onions, and onions. Cook, stirring, for 2 minutes, then add the sirloin strips to the pan. Sprinkle the meat with the curry powder and ginger. Cook over medium heat, stirring and turning, until the meat is lightly browned, about 5 minutes. Add the coconut milk or water. Lower the heat to a simmer and cover the pan. Cook for 10–15 minutes, or until the meat is tender.

Zesty Fish Fillets

Yield: 6 servings

"If farmers do not cultivate their fields, the people in the town will die of hunger."

—GUINEAN PROVERB

3 tablespoons butter or margarine, melted
2 pounds fish (bass, catfish, cod, orange roughy, salmon, or tuna) filleted, in 6 portions about 1 inch thick
2 tablespoons orange juice
2 teaspoons grated orange zest
1 teaspoon salt
½ teaspoon ground nutmeg
½ teaspoon black pepper

Preheat the oven to 350 degrees. Using 1 tablespoon of the melted butter, lightly grease a large baking pan. Place the fish in a single layer in the pan. In a small bowl, mix together the remaining 2 tablespoons butter, the orange juice, orange zest, salt, nutmeg, and pepper. Pour the sauce over the fish. Bake for 10–15 minutes. Do not overcook.

Stuffed Fillets in Cheese Sauce

Yield: 6 servings

"Our nettlesome task is to discover how to organize our strength into compelling power."

—MARTIN LUTHER KING, JR.

FISH:

2 pounds fish (bass, catfish, cod, orange roughy, salmon, or tuna) filleted, in 6 portions about 1 inch thick

4 tablespoons butter, melted

2 tablespoons lemon juice

1 teaspoon salt

1 teaspoon black pepper

1 teaspoon sweet paprika

STUFFING:

1 cup dry breadcrumbs

½ cup melted butter

¼ teaspoon salt

⅛ teaspoon black pepper

2 tablespoons chopped parsley

CHEESE SAUCE:

2 tablespoons butter

2 tablespoons all-purpose flour

1½ cups milk

2 cups grated sharp cheddar cheese

½ teaspoon salt

½ teaspoon black pepper

½ teaspoon dry mustard

⅛ teaspoon sweet paprika

Preheat the oven to 325 degrees. Dip the fish into the melted butter until well coated. Set aside. In a small bowl, combine all the ingredients for the bread stuffing. Spread each fillet with a small amount of the stuffing. Starting at the widest end, carefully roll the fillets into bundles. Secure with a toothpick. Place the stuffed fillets in a 13 × 9 × 2-inch baking dish. Sprinkle the lemon juice, salt, pepper, and paprika over the fillets. To prepare the cheese sauce, melt the butter in a small saucepan over medium-low heat. Add the flour, stir, and let the mixture bubble gently about 1 minute. Slowly add the milk, stirring constantly, and let the sauce heat and thicken slightly before adding the cheese, salt, pepper, mustard, and paprika. Stir until the cheese has melted and the mixture is smooth and thick. Pour the cheese sauce over the fillets and bake, uncovered, for 20–30 minutes.

New Orleans Catfish

Yield: 8 servings

"Negro action can be decisive. I say that we ourselves have the power to end the terror and to win for ourselves peace and security throughout the land."

—PAUL ROBESON, SINGER, ACTOR,
POLITICAL ACTIVIST

2 tablespoons dried or ground thyme
2 cloves garlic, peeled
1 tablespoon sweet paprika
1 tablespoon white pepper
1 small onion, peeled
1 tablespoon black pepper
1 tablespoon salt
½ teaspoon ground red pepper (cayenne)
1 tablespoon dried oregano
3 bay leaves
8 9–12 ounce catfish fillets
1 stick butter or margarine

Preheat the oven to 375 degrees. In a blender, grind the thyme, garlic, paprika, white pepper, onion, black pepper, salt, cayenne pepper, oregano, and bay leaves together. Place the mixture on a plate. Coat one side of the catfish fillets with the mixture. Melt the butter in a medium skillet. Place the coated side of 2 or 3 fillets in the butter and cook for 3 minutes over moderate heat. Place the fillets, coated side up, in a large baking pan in one layer. Repeat with remaining fillets. Bake for 15 minutes. Do not overcook.

4

Vegetables and Side Dishes

UJAMAA
(Cooperative Economics)
To build and maintain our own stores, shops, and other businesses, and to profit from them together.

I don't know of any business that didn't start with a dream. Taking care of business means making your dreams a reality. Cooperative economics is all about helping others fulfill their dreams while you help yourself and your community. There's a saying from the sixties that sums it all up: "Buy black."

African-Americans have a long and creative business tradition. During the years we were enslaved, many African-American men and women were allowed to earn money by selling their crafts, their musical ability, and their expertise with food. There are several stories about slaves who earned enough money to buy their freedom.

They earned this money through their ability to use their skills and conduct business under the worst possible conditions.

During the long years of segregation, the black business community flourished out of necessity, the mother of invention. We opened businesses that catered to the needs of our community. Community members shopped at the stores owned by people they went to school and church with. Business owners helped with community projects large and small. Black business owners and their patrons worked cooperatively with one another for the betterment of everyone.

The spirit of our ancestors lives on in the large number of black-owned businesses that open their doors every year. In my hometown, there are several McDonald's, including one that is owned by an industrious African-American couple who decided to take a gamble and buy into the franchise. I enjoy "taking a break" anytime at their restaurant because I know what they had to go through to establish themselves as business owners. I've enjoyed watching them succeed, and they are generous with their support of our community.

African-Americans have broken down many barriers in the business world to create companies that assist, uplift, and inspire. My favorite kinds of businesses are those that are beneficial to others, ones that celebrate the true spirit of cooperative economics. For instance, African-American bookstores are what I call an *ujamaa* business. Inside a bookstore you can introduce people to the knowledge and ideas that are contained between the covers of a book. You can educate, enlighten, and uplift your customers and still make a living. You assist those who write by promoting and selling their work. You introduce your customers to information about their culture and history they may not encounter anywhere else. You're a business, but with a special service.

It's possible to start something from a little of nothing. The key is to start small, work hard, allow your dreams to grow, enlist the support of your community, and return that support whenever you're able to. After all, success runs in our race.

Creole-style Green Beans

Yield: 8 servings

"I would never be of any service to anyone as a slave."

—NAT TURNER, REVOLUTIONARY

1 10-ounce package frozen French-style green beans
2 tablespoons vegetable oil
2 stalks celery, diced
1 green bell pepper, ribs and seeds removed, diced
1 small onion, diced
1 28-ounce can whole tomatoes, drained and coarsely
   chopped
½ teaspoon sugar
⅛ teaspoon salt
⅛ teaspoon black pepper

Cook the green beans according to the package directions and set aside. Heat the oil in a large skillet. Sauté the celery, bell pepper, and onion until tender. Add the tomatoes and simmer, uncovered, on low heat, for 15 minutes, or until most of the liquid has evaporated. Add the sugar, salt, pepper, and green beans to the skillet. Simmer for 5 minutes.

Green Beans with Okra

Yield: 4 servings

I had never thought of preparing green beans with okra until the host of a talk show told me about her family's recipe. All I can say is: Don't knock it until you've tried it!

4 slices lean bacon, cut into ½-inch squares
½ cup chopped green onions
1 10-ounce package frozen green beans or 1 pound fresh green beans, washed, snapped, and with strings removed
½ cup water
8–12 baby okra, fresh or frozen (thawed)
1 teaspoon salt
¼ teaspoon black pepper
1½ teaspoons red wine vinegar

In a large skillet, fry the bacon squares until brown and crisp, then place them on a paper towel to drain. Sauté the green onions in the bacon fat for about 2–3 minutes, until they are soft but not brown. Add the green beans to the skillet, stirring them until they are well coated with the bacon fat. Add the water and the okra. Cover the pan tightly. Cook over low heat for 15–20 minutes, or until the vegetables are tender. Sprinkle with the salt and pepper, stir in the vinegar, and remove from the heat. Place the green beans and okra in a serving dish and sprinkle with the bacon.

Broccoli with Cream Sauce

Yield: 8 servings

"It is quite easy to shout slogans, to sign manifestos, but it is quite a different matter to build, manage, command, spend days and nights seeking the solution of problems."

—PATRICE LUMUMBA,
FIRST PRIME MINISTER OF THE CONGO, NOW ZAIRE

2 10-ounce packages frozen broccoli
1 10¾-ounce can cream of chicken soup
½ cup mayonnaise
¼ cup dry breadcrumbs
½ teaspoon sweet paprika

Preheat the oven to 300 degrees. Place the packages of frozen broccoli in a pan of cold water until defrosted—this will make it easier to separate the individual stalks. Drain broccoli, dry well on paper towels, and place in a baking dish. In a small bowl, mix together the soup and mayonnaise. Pour the mixture over the broccoli stalks. Sprinkle with the breadcrumbs and paprika. Bake, uncovered, for 30 minutes.

Spinach and Mushroom Casserole

Yield: 8 servings

"No race can prosper till it learns that there is as much dignity in tilling a field as there is in writing a poem."

—BOOKER T. WASHINGTON, EDUCATOR

2 10-ounce packages frozen chopped spinach
6 slices bacon
4 green onions, chopped
1 small onion, chopped
¼ cup breadcrumbs
1 cup sliced mushrooms
1 teaspoon salt
1 teaspoon black pepper
1 teaspoon butter or margarine

Preheat the oven to 350 degrees. Cook the spinach according to package directions. Drain and set aside. In a medium skillet, fry the bacon until crisp, then place the slices on a paper towel–covered plate to drain. Sauté the onions in the bacon fat until soft but not brown. Crumble the bacon and add to the pan along with the breadcrumbs, mushrooms, spinach, salt, and pepper. Mix all ingredients well. Grease a casserole dish with the butter or margarine. Spoon the spinach mixture into the casserole dish and bake, uncovered, for 20 minutes.

Spicy Collards and Cabbage

Yield: 8 servings

"Like many, I found that the best therapy in the world is work. Lots of it!"

—JOHNETTA B. COLE, Ph.D.,

FIRST WOMAN PRESIDENT OF SPELMAN COLLEGE

1 bunch (about 2 pounds) collard greens
4 cups water
½ pound bacon, cut into 1-inch pieces
1 large onion, sliced
1½ teaspoons salt
1 teaspoon sugar
½ teaspoon ground red pepper (cayenne)
1 teaspoon black pepper
1 large head cabbage, cut into 8 wedges
2 tablespoons butter or margarine

Cut the tough stems and yellow leaves from the collard greens and discard. Gently rub the leaves with your fingers under warm running water. Cut the greens into large pieces. Let the leaves soak in warm, salted water for 10 minutes. Rinse with cool water and drain in a colander.

In a large pot, bring the water to a boil. Add the collard greens, bacon, onion, salt, sugar, red pepper, and black pepper. Reduce heat, cover, and simmer, stirring occasionally, for 1 hour. Add the cabbage and the butter or margarine. Simmer for another 15 minutes, or until the vegetables are tender.

New-style Collard Greens

Yield: 8 servings

This recipe greatly reduces the fat normally added to collard greens, but it keeps the flavor.

2 bunches (about 4 pounds) collard greens
6 cups water
2 pounds smoked turkey wings, cut at the joints
2 teaspoons salt
1 or 2 dried red peppers or ½ teaspoon ground red
   pepper (cayenne)
1 clove garlic, mashed
½ teaspoon sugar
1 tablespoon olive oil

Cut the tough stems and yellow leaves from the collard greens and discard. Gently rub the leaves with your fingers under warm running water. Cut the greens into large pieces. Let the leaves soak in warm, salted water for 10 minutes. Rinse with cool water and drain in a colander.

In a large pot, bring the water to a boil. Add the collard greens, smoked turkey wings, salt, red pepper, garlic, sugar, and olive oil. Reduce heat, cover, and simmer over low heat for 1½–2 hours, or until the greens are tender. Stir occasionally and add hot water to cover the greens as needed.

Muhindi (Corn)

Yield: 8 servings

"At the bottom of education, at the bottom of politics, even at the bottom of religion, there must be for our race economic independence."

—BOOKER T. WASHINGTON, EDUCATOR

1 8-ounce package cream cheese, softened
⅔ cup milk
2 tablespoons butter or margarine
1 teaspoon onion salt
2 15¼-ounce cans whole-kernel corn, drained

Combine the cream cheese, milk, butter or margarine, and onion salt in a small saucepan. Over low heat, stirring often, cook until the cheese melts and the ingredients are well blended. Stir in the corn. Stirring constantly, cook for 3 to 5 minutes, or until the corn is heated.

Festive Corn

Yield: 6 servings

"We must not only be able to black boots, but to make them."

—FREDERICK DOUGLASS,
STATESMAN, PUBLISHER, JOURNALIST

3 tablespoons butter or margarine
4 tablespoons chopped onion
1 medium green bell pepper, seeds and ribs removed, chopped
2 tablespoons all-purpose flour
2 cups fresh or frozen (thawed) or 2 15¼-ounce cans whole-kernel corn, drained
2 cups tomato juice
1 teaspoon salt
¼ teaspoon black pepper
2 tablespoons sugar
2 egg yolks, slightly beaten

In a large skillet, melt the butter or margarine. Sauté the onion and bell pepper until tender. Add the flour and mix until well blended. Add the corn, tomato juice, salt, pepper, and sugar. Mix well. Stir in the egg yolks and cook over low heat for 2–3 minutes, until heated through.

Honeyed Beets

Yield: 6 servings

"A man's bread and butter is only insured when he works for it."

—MARCUS GARVEY, FOUNDER OF THE UNIVERSAL
NEGRO IMPROVEMENT ASSOCIATION

1½ **tablespoons cornstarch**
½ **teaspoon salt**
2 **tablespoons water**
3 **tablespoons white vinegar**
⅓ **cup honey**
2 **tablespoons butter**
1 **16-ounce can sliced beets, drained**

Combine the cornstarch and salt in a small saucepan. Add the water, mixing until smoothly blended. Add the vinegar, honey, and butter. Stirring constantly, cook over low heat until the mixture thickens. Add the beets and cook until they are heated through.

Sesame Potatoes

Yield: 8 servings

"It is the fool whose own tomatoes are sold to him."

—AKAN PROVERB

1 tablespoon butter or margarine
8 medium baking potatoes
¾ cup sesame seeds
1 stick butter or margarine, melted
1½ teaspoons salt
1 teaspoon sweet paprika

Preheat the oven to 400 degrees. Grease a large baking dish with 1 tablespoon butter or margarine. Peel the potatoes and cut into 1 inch-thick crosswise slices. Place the slices in a bowl of cold water. Sprinkle the sesame seeds on a sheet of waxed paper. Dry the potato slices, then dip them into the melted butter or margarine and press one side down on the sesame seeds. Place the slices, seed side up, in the greased baking dish. Sprinkle with the salt and paprika. Bake for 40 minutes, or until done.

Orange-glazed Sweet Potatoes

Yield: 8 servings

"Treat your guest as a guest for two days; on the third day, give him a hoe!"

—SWAHILI FOLK SAYING

8 medium sweet potatoes
1 teaspoon salt

GLAZE:
2 tablespoons butter or margarine
1 tablespoon orange zest
¾ cup dark corn syrup

Scrub the sweet potatoes to remove dirt. Fill a large pot with water, add the potatoes and salt, cover, and boil the potatoes for 30–40 minutes, or until tender when pierced with a fork. After the potatoes have cooled, peel them and cut them in half lengthwise. Place them, cut side down, in a large, shallow baking dish.

Preheat the oven to 350 degrees. In a small saucepan, combine the butter or margarine, orange zest, and corn syrup. Bring the ingredients to a boil, stirring constantly. Pour the glaze over the sweet potatoes. Bake for 30 minutes, basting the potatoes occasionally with the syrup.

Creamy Sweet Potatoes

Yield: 6 servings

"The society we seek to build among black people, then, is not a capitalist one. It is a society in which the spirit of community and humanistic love prevail."

—STOKELY CARMICHAEL (KWAME TURE),
POLITICAL ACTIVIST

6 large sweet potatoes
½ cup light cream
3 tablespoons butter or margarine
½ teaspoon salt
¼ teaspoon ground nutmeg
⅛ teaspoon black pepper

Scrub the sweet potatoes to remove dirt. Place the sweet potatoes in a large pot and cover with cold water. Cover the pot and cook the potatoes for 30–40 minutes, or until tender when pierced with a fork. Remove the potatoes from the pot and set aside to cool; then peel and lightly mash them. In a large bowl, using a mixer, combine the potatoes, cream, butter or margarine, salt, nutmeg, and pepper and continue whipping until the potatoes are smooth and fluffy.

West African Potato Foo Foo

Yield: 8 servings

"It is poor working-class wisdom to fight big business for economic justice on the industrial field and vote for it on the political."

—A. PHILIP RANDOLPH,
FOUNDER OF THE BROTHERHOOD
OF SLEEPING CAR PORTERS

3 pounds potatoes (sweet or white potatoes or yams or a combination)
1 tablespoon butter

Wash the potatoes to remove any dirt. Place them in a large pot and fill with water. Cover the pot and cook the potatoes for 30–40 minutes, or until tender when pierced with a fork. Remove the potatoes and set aside to cool; then peel and cut them into small pieces. In a large bowl or using a mixer, mash the potatoes and butter together. Do not add any liquid, since the *foo foo* should be of a thick consistency.

Saffron Rice

Yield: 6 servings

"Man cannot live by profit alone."

—JAMES BALDWIN, AUTHOR

2 cups canned coconut milk
⅛ teaspoon saffron
¼ teaspoon sugar
2 cloves
2 ½-inch sticks of cinnamon
¼ teaspoon salt
1 cup long-grain or short-grain rice

Pour the coconut milk into a medium saucepan. Stir in the saffron, sugar, cloves, cinnamon, and salt. Bring the ingredients to a boil, then add the rice. Cover tightly and turn the heat to low. Cook for 15–20 minutes without removing the lid, or until liquid is absorbed. Remove cloves and cinnamon sticks before serving.

Lemony Rice

Yield: 6 servings

There's nothing like the bright flavor of lemon to perk up a holiday meal.

1 cup long-grain rice
2 tablespoons butter or margarine
1 clove garlic, mashed
⅛ teaspoon dried turmeric
½ cup lemon juice
1½ cups water
½ teaspoon salt
½ teaspoon black pepper
2 green onions, finely chopped

Wash the rice in a sieve under cool, running water. Set aside to drain. Melt the butter or margarine in a medium saucepan. Add the garlic and sauté until lightly browned. Add the rice, turmeric, lemon juice, water, salt, and pepper. Bring the ingredients to a boil, then reduce heat to a simmer and cover. Simmer for 15 minutes without uncovering. Serve the rice sprinkled with the green onions.

5

Cooking for Company

NIA
(*Purpose*)

To make our collective vocation the building and developing
of our community in order to restore our people to their
traditional greatness.

One of the best ways I've found of putting the Kwanzaa principle of *nia* into action is immersing oneself in a community project that fits in with one's own goals and interests. I love reading and writing: therefore, the projects I focus on in my community are literacy based. I'm more committed to these projects than to others I've undertaken (although they were also good causes) because books are important in my personal and professional life. I devote myself to causes involving children and their parents because I feel that "in order to restore our people to their traditional greatness" we must work with our children now to correct the errors of the past and to ensure that our cultural heritage continues.

As with most everybody, my time is limited, and sometimes seems nonexistent. There are a few ways you can make time for a purpose. If you go to church four or five Sundays a month, maybe one of those days could be devoted instead to putting what you know into practice in your community. Television steals a lot of time. An hour in the evening could be spent assisting a neighborhood child with homework. I once had as many excuses as anyone else, but as the saying goes, "If you want to get something done, ask a busy person."

It's a struggle raising a child even in the best of circumstances. But raising a child alone, on one income, with little or no child support, puts many single parents below the poverty line. With three out of five African-American children being raised by a single parent, our purpose as a community should be the emotional, spiritual, and cultural well-being of our children. There is an African proverb that says, "It takes a whole village to raise a child." We must organize our efforts as a community to watch over the village children.

There are several wonderful organizations that need volunteers and that are terrific resources in starting any neighborhood effort to help our children.

Marian Wright Edelman, founder of the Children's Defense Fund, is a lawyer and a lobbyist. Her clients are the poor children of America. The Children's Defense Fund (CDF) was founded in Washington, D.C., in 1973 to provide systematic and long-range assistance to children and to make their needs a matter of public policy.

Edelman was taught from an early age to be active

in her community. "Service was as much a part of my upbringing as eating breakfast and going to school. It wasn't something that you do in your spare time. Helping others had the highest value," says Edelman. In 1960, she was arrested when she participated in the huge sit-in in Atlanta, Georgia, at City Hall. The experience convinced her that more civil rights attorneys were needed. She applied to Yale University Law School and spent her spring break in Mississippi registering voters. In 1965, she became the first African-American woman to be admitted to the bar in Mississippi. While working in Mississippi, Edelman realized that in order to effectively change the system she needed to change federal policy.

"The issue for me when I moved to Washington in 1968 was how could one provide a countervoice to the powerful in order to see poor people have a chance to help themselves and their children," Edelman says. "If you're serious about an educated workforce and you're serious about giving kids that early foundation, then you can't throw them out there into cheap baby-sitting. We've got to invest in it and that's going to cost a little money. And the issue isn't whether we're going to spend the money, it's when and how much. Because you'll pay for them in prison or you'll pay for them in day care."

Another organization that has been an active force for change in the African-American community is Men Against Destruction Defending Against Drugs and Social Disorder, MAD DADS, Inc. John Foster started MAD DADS in 1989 in Omaha, Nebraska, after his son was beaten by a gang. Foster joined with religious and community leaders in forming an organization that provides role models for black youths. "We knew that we had to take action. And there's something spiritually strong about black men coming together for a common purpose," says Eddie Staton, one of Foster's partners. "Whether it's on the basketball court or on the streets, we're a force."

The organization now has thirty-two chapters around the United States, is multiracial, and includes moms, too. Using structure, love, and attention, volunteers patrol neighborhood streets during the weekends to talk with young men. MAD DADS also offers a training program that teaches everything from parenting skills to black history. "What we may think of as the worst kid can be reached if you do it the right way," says Staton. "It's important that we understand our culture and be proud."

Organizations like the Children's Defense Fund and MAD DADS, Inc., prod us into action by awakening us to the horrifying problems that our children face daily. We can change things if we choose to do it. As a community, we must look out for those who are unable to look out for themselves. Our children are our future. Get involved. If you can't commit the time, send money. If you don't have the money, commit the time. Make a sacrifice for the future. Supporting organizations that nurture children gives us a chance to shape tomorrow's African-American community today.

Breakfast

Oven-baked Pancake

Yield: 12 servings

This recipe provides a fruity breakfast feast for a crowd, but is easy to prepare.

12 eggs
3 cups milk
3 cups all-purpose flour
1½ teaspoons salt
1½ sticks margarine or butter, melted
3 cups shredded Swiss or Monterey Jack cheese
1 20-ounce can sliced apples
Powdered sugar (optional)

Preheat the oven to 425 degrees. In a large bowl, beat the eggs for about 2 minutes, then add the milk, flour, and salt. Beat until well blended. Pour the melted margarine or butter into a 13 × 9 × 2-inch baking dish. Pour the egg mixture into the dish. Bake for 25 minutes, or until the sides of the pancake are golden brown and puffy. Remove the dish from the oven. Sprinkle with the cheese. Arrange the apples in the center of the pancake. Sprinkle with powdered sugar, if desired.

Zanzibar Pancakes

Yield: 10 pancakes

Zanzibar is a corruption of an Arab word that means "the coast of the blacks." These pancakes are delightful for breakfast and are perfect for vegetarian guests. The toasted sesame seeds give the pancakes a slightly crunchy texture.

1 teaspoon active dry yeast
1 cup warm water
1 teaspoon sugar
1 cup all-purpose flour
⅔ cup milk
½ cup vegetable oil
3 tablespoons toasted sesame seeds (see page 129)
Jam or jelly

In a small bowl, dissolve the yeast in the warm water. Stir in the sugar and put the uncovered mixture in a warm place until it starts to foam, about 5 minutes. If it doesn't foam, the yeast is too old. Discard the mixture and start the process over again with a fresh package of yeast. Sift the flour into a large bowl. Using a large spoon, make a well in the center of the flour. Stir the yeast mixture into the well. Then, stirring constantly, slowly add the milk. Mix until the ingredients are smooth and thick and run slowly from the spoon. If too thick, add warm water, a tablespoon at a time, to the batter.

Heat 1 tablespoon of the oil in a skillet over medium heat. Spoon in the batter until it spreads to form a pancake about the size of a saucer. Cook until the pancake is golden brown on the bottom, about 1 minute. Sprinkle a few drops of oil on the pancake and turn it over to cook on the other side. Sprinkle the top with a few of the toasted sesame seeds. Repeat the process with the remaining batter, adding oil as necessary to prevent the pancakes from sticking. Serve warm with jam or jelly.

Company French Toast
Yield: 12 servings

If you have a house full of company, this is the perfect breakfast, since you can prepare it the night before and pop it into the oven the next morning.

2 sticks butter or margarine, melted
1 cup orange juice
¾ cup honey
9 eggs
1 teaspoon ground cinnamon
1 teaspoon ground nutmeg
12 slices of bread, at least 1 inch thick (Italian bread or
    Texas toast)

Pour the melted margarine or butter into 2 shallow baking pans. Using an electric mixer or hand beater, combine the orange juice, honey, eggs, cinnamon, and nutmeg until well blended and foamy. Dip the bread into the egg mixture. Place the bread slices in the pans in a single layer. Drizzle the remaining egg mixture over the bread. Cover the pans and refrigerate at least 1 hour or overnight.

When ready to cook, preheat the oven to 450 degrees. Bake the French toast, uncovered, for 10 minutes, or until the bottoms are golden brown. Turn the slices and bake another 6–8 minutes, or until the bottoms are golden brown.

Breakfast-in-a-Dish

Yield: 6 servings

"Black people know how to save our children. Our little children are the most intuitive, the brightest kids. To reach them we just have to get back to basics."

—NELLIE COOKE, EDUCATOR

2 6-ounce packages bulk spicy pork sausage
1 small onion, chopped
3 cups frozen shredded hash brown potatoes, thawed
½ teaspoon salt
½ teaspoon black pepper
1½ cups shredded Swiss cheese
6 eggs

Preheat the oven to 350 degrees. In a large skillet over medium heat, sauté the sausage and onion, stirring, until the sausage is brown and the onion is golden brown. Drain off the fat. Stir in the potatoes, salt, and pepper. Cook for 2–3 minutes, then remove from the heat. Stir in the cheese. Spread the mixture in a large ungreased 11 × 7 × 1½-inch baking dish. With the back of a large spoon, make 6 indentations in the mixture. Break 1 egg into each indentation. Bake, uncovered, 20–25 minutes, or until the eggs are done.

Appetizers and Salads

Soul food Dip

Yield: 6 cups

"On the way to one's beloved, there are no hills."
—AFRICAN PROVERB

2 tablespoons butter or margarine
½ medium onion, diced
½ cup diced celery
1 10-ounce package frozen chopped turnip greens
1 teaspoon salt
1 teaspoon black pepper
¼ teaspoon grated lemon zest
1 10¾-ounce can cream of mushroom soup, undiluted
1 3-ounce can sliced mushrooms, drained, or ½ cup
  fresh mushrooms, chopped
1 6-ounce package cream cheese
½ teaspoon garlic powder
1 teaspoon Worcestershire sauce
5 drops hot sauce

Melt the butter or margarine in a large saucepan. Over medium heat, sauté the onion and celery until the onion is golden brown and the celery is tender, about 10 minutes. In a small pan, cook the turnip greens according to the package directions. Drain well and season with the salt and pepper. In a blender or food processor, grind the turnip greens and lemon zest together until smooth. Add the turnip greens mixture, mushroom soup, mushrooms, cheese, garlic powder, Worcestershire sauce, and hot sauce to the sautéed onion and celery. Stirring constantly, cook the mixture over medium heat until the cheese is melted and the ingredients are blended. Serve warm with Sesame Seed Wafers (see page 127).

Bacon and Cheese Delights

Yield: 15 servings

"The dog has four feet, but he does not walk them on four roads."

—HAITIAN PROVERB

1 cup shredded Monterey Jack cheese
8 slices bacon, cooked and crumbled
3 tablespoons mayonnaise
½ tablespoon mild salsa
1 tablespoon grated onion
½ teaspoon salt
½ teaspoon dried or ground thyme
10 slices day-old sandwich bread, crusts removed

Preheat the oven to 325 degrees. Mix the cheese, crumbled bacon, mayonnaise, salsa, onion, salt, and thyme until well blended. Spread the mixture over the bread slices. Carefully cut each slice into thirds. Bake on a cookie sheet for 10 minutes, or until the cheese has melted.

Crowd-pleasing Coleslaw

Yield: 25 servings

"If a man is called to be a street sweeper, he should sweep streets even as Michelangelo painted or Beethoven composed music or Shakespeare wrote poetry."

—MARTIN LUTHER KING, JR.

5 pounds cabbage, shredded
½ cup minced onions
2 cups shredded carrots
1 tablespoon salt
1 tablespoon black pepper
1 quart mayonnaise or salad dressing, or to taste

In a large container, mix the cabbage, onions, carrots, salt, and pepper. Refrigerate. Just before serving, mix in the mayonnaise or salad dressing until the ingredients are well coated.

Power Pasta with Garlic Dressing

Yield: 12 servings

"I had to practically hypnotize myself into thinking
I was going to be a success."

—JOHN SINGLETON, FILM DIRECTOR

2 16-ounce packages mixed frozen broccoli and
   cauliflower florets, or 1 each
12 ounces ziti or macaroni, cooked and drained
2 carrots, shredded
2 stalks celery, thinly sliced
¼ cup sliced pitted ripe olives
3 tablespoons grated Parmesan cheese
1 cup grated Swiss cheese
¼ cup white wine
1 red bell pepper, seeds and ribs removed, chopped
1 green bell pepper, seeds and ribs removed, chopped
1 tablespoon salt
1 tablespoon black pepper
Garlic Dressing (recipe follows)

Cook the broccoli and cauliflower according to the package directions. In a large salad bowl, combine the cooked vegetables with the ziti or macaroni, carrots, celery, olives, cheeses, wine, bell peppers, salt, and pepper. Toss with the Garlic Dressing. Serve at room temperature or chilled.

Garlic Dressing

1 clove garlic, peeled
1 tomato, quartered
6 sprigs parsley
1½ teaspoons Dijon mustard
2 tablespoons red wine vinegar
½ teaspoon salt
½ cup vegetable oil
⅓ cup olive oil

In a food processor or blender, grind the garlic, tomato, parsley, mustard, vinegar, and salt. Continue blending ingredients while slowly adding the oils, until the mixture is smooth and well blended.

Main Dishes

Spicy Beef and Rice Casserole

Yield: 12 servings

This casserole is easy to prepare and transport to a Kwanzaa community supper.

2 pounds cooked ground beef
2 cups cooked rice
1 large green bell pepper, seeds and ribs removed, diced
2 16-ounce cans stewed tomatoes, drained
2 teaspoons salt
1 teaspoon black pepper
1 teaspoon dry mustard
2 teaspoons dried or ground oregano
2 teaspoons chili powder
1 cup shredded cheddar cheese

Preheat oven to 350 degrees. In a 13 × 9 × 2-inch baking dish, combine all the ingredients except the cheddar cheese. Sprinkle the cheese on top. Bake the casserole for 30 minutes.

Seafood Casserole

Yield: 16 servings

This casserole can be made a day ahead of time and refrigerated. Simply follow the recipe up to the point where the prepared ingredients are poured into the casserole dishes and refrigerate them. Do not sprinkle on the breadcrumbs or bake the casseroles until you are ready to serve the meal.

2 sticks butter or margarine
1 pound fresh mushrooms, sliced
2 tablespoons all-purpose flour
3 cups evaporated milk, warmed
2 green onions, chopped
½ teaspoon ground mace
2 tablespoons minced parsley
1 teaspoon salt
1 tablespoon hot sauce
4 egg yolks
1 cup mayonnaise or salad dressing
2 pounds lump crabmeat
2 pounds shrimp, peeled, deveined, and boiled 3 minutes
1 cup dry breadcrumbs

In a large skillet, melt 2 tablespoons of the butter or margarine. Over medium heat, sauté the mushrooms for about a minute, then remove them from the skillet and set aside. Over low heat, melt the remaining butter or margarine in the skillet. Slowly blend in the flour, stirring until smooth. Add the warm milk, green onions, mace, parsley, salt, and hot sauce. Stirring constantly, cook until the mixture has thickened. In a small bowl, mix 2 tablespoons of the flour mixture from the skillet with the egg yolks. Pour the egg yolk mixture into the skillet. Stir until the ingredients are well blended, about 3–5 minutes. Remove the sauce from the heat. Add the mayonnaise or dressing, the mushrooms, crabmeat, and shrimp to the skillet. Mix well. Butter 2 2½-quart casserole dishes. Divide the seafood mixture evenly between them.

When ready to cook the casseroles, preheat the oven to 350 degrees. If the casseroles have been refrigerated, let them come to room temperature. Sprinkle the breadcrumbs over each casserole. Bake for 20–25 minutes, or until the casseroles are bubbling hot.

Deluxe Chicken Dinner

Yield: 12 servings

This all-in-one-pot recipe makes a fantastic dish for the *karamu* feast.

1 bunch celery, chopped, with leaves
1 large onion, chopped
4 cups cubed cooked chicken
5 cups chicken broth
2 cups brown or white rice
1 tablespoon salt
1 tablespoon poultry seasoning
1 tablespoon dried or ground sage
2 bay leaves
¼ teaspoon hot sauce
½ stick butter or margarine
5 carrots, cut into ½-inch rounds
1 large green bell pepper, seeds and ribs removed, sliced into strips

In a large Dutch oven or heavy kettle, mix all the ingredients except the carrots and bell pepper. Cover and cook for 35 minutes over low heat. Stir in the carrots and bell pepper and cook for another 40 minutes, or until the vegetables are tender and the rice is cooked. Discard bay leaves before serving.

Ugandan Vegetable Casserole

Yield: 12 servings

"In search of my mother's garden, I found my own."

—ALICE WALKER, AUTHOR AND POET

4 tablespoons vegetable oil
1 medium onion, sliced into rings
1 large eggplant, unpeeled and diced
1 red bell pepper, seeds and ribs removed, diced
2 cloves garlic, mashed
1 10-ounce package frozen spinach, thawed, or 1 pound fresh spinach, cleaned and chopped
2 medium zucchini, peeled and sliced
2 medium tomatoes, cut into wedges
1 teaspoon salt
1 teaspoon black pepper

Pour the oil into a large pot and, over medium heat, allow the oil to heat for 3–5 minutes. Add the onion and sauté, turning, for 2–3 minutes. Add the vegetables in the order listed, cooking and turning each for 1–2 minutes before adding the next ingredient. Season the vegetables with salt and pepper. Reduce the heat to low and cover the pot. Simmer for 10–15 minutes, or until all the vegetables are tender.

Desserts

Gingersnap Cakes
Yield: 16 servings

These refrigerator cakes are a "snap" to prepare.

2 sticks butter or margarine, softened
2 cups powdered sugar
4 eggs
2 teaspoons vanilla extract
2 cups crushed pineapple
6 bananas, peeled and sliced into rounds
1 cup chopped almonds
1½ cups heavy cream, whipped, or 12 ounces whipped topping
1 pound gingersnaps, finely crushed

Using a mixer, in a large bowl, cream the butter or margarine and sugar until smooth. Beat in the eggs and vanilla until the mixture is well blended and creamy. Stir in the pineapple, bananas, almonds, and half the whipped cream or topping. Spread one-third of the gingersnap crumbs evenly over the bottoms of 2 13 × 9 × 2-inch baking dishes. Pour the cream mixture over the crumbs in each dish. Sprinkle another one-third of the crumbs over the cream mixture. Spread the remaining whipped cream over the crumbs. Garnish with the remaining crumbs. Chill overnight.

Apple Crisps

Yield: 12 servings

"Start with what you know and build with what
you have."

—KWAME NKRUMAH, FORMER PRESIDENT OF GHANA

4 20-ounce cans sliced apples
2 cups sugar
1 stick butter or margarine, softened and cut up
1 tablespoon all-purpose flour
1½ tablespoons ground cinnamon
1½ tablespoons ground nutmeg
2 teaspoons lemon juice

TOPPING:
3 cups all-purpose flour
1½ sticks butter or margarine, softened
1 cup sugar
2 tablespoons light brown sugar

Preheat the oven to 400 degrees. In a large bowl, gently
mix the apples, sugar, butter or margarine, flour, cinnamon, nutmeg, and lemon juice until the apples are well
coated. Place the apple mixture in 2 13 × 9 × 2-inch
baking dishes. In a large bowl, using a fork, combine all
the topping ingredients until well blended. Press spoon-
fuls of the topping over the apples until they are evenly
covered. Bake the crisps for 45 minutes, or until bubbly
hot and the topping is golden brown.

6

Breads and Desserts

KUUMBA
(Creativity)
To do always as much as we can, in the way we can, in order
to leave our community more beautiful and beneficial than
it was when we inherited it.

Before I began studying the *nguzo saba* principle of *kuumba*, I did not consider all the ways one can creatively benefit a community or the impact that African-American art, music, dance, and literature have had on my own life. There are far too many African-American artists to describe in one essay; however, I wanted to honor a few whose work has been a special inspiration to me, and others.

Jacob Lawrence preserved a part of African-American history and culture through his art. Lawrence's work included a series of paintings by him and narratives by his wife, artist Gwendolyn Knight. His paintings about the lives of Harriet Tubman, Toussaint-Louverture, Frederick Douglass, and his series about the great migration brought history alive visually. Another artist, James Van Der Zee, used his camera to capture a vibrant Harlem community from 1920 to 1980. Without Van Der Zee's images, many people would have never seen a glimpse of the elegant and community-oriented Harlem of the past.

African-American writers have allowed us to use our imaginations to re-create the worlds their words paint. Their works have inspired and motivated the African-American community in a special way. The passion of Richard Wright and James Baldwin burn through the pages of their books. The poetry of Claude McKay, Langston Hughes, Amiri Baraka, Nikki Giovanni, Haki Madhubuti, Mari Evans, Sonia Sanchez, and Gil Scott-Heron expose the soul of a people in the midst of a revolution. Maya Angelou stood before the world and poetically declared a new day. Playwrights Lorraine Hansberry, August Wilson, and Charles Fuller dramatically represent the joys and struggles of African-American life.

I don't think this cookbook would be complete without writing about the creative genius of artist and scientist Dr. George Washington Carver. In an autobiographical sketch, Carver wrote, "From a child I had an inordinate desire for knowledge and especially music, painting, flowers and the sciences." Carver was not only a gifted artist but a brilliant scientist as well. His discoveries created a new economy for Southern farmers. His work at the Tuskegee Institute with peanuts, soybeans, and sweet potatoes has made him one of the most famous African-American scientists in history. But Carver had the soul of an artist, and his creative genius was his ability to make something out of items that looked "useless"—wallboard from pine cones, banana stems, and peanut shells; synthetic marble from sawdust; woven rugs from okra stalks; 118 different products from the sweet potato and more than 300 from the peanut! Carver once said, "Of course, it has always been the one great ideal of my life to be the greatest good to the greatest number of my people possible, and to this end I have been preparing myself for these many years."

Artists provide a special service to the African-American community. Whatever the medium may be, art uplifts, informs, and enriches.

Garlic Cheese Biscuits

Yield: 12 servings

These cheddar cheese biscuits are easy to prepare, and the garlic enhances the flavor.

½ **stick butter or margarine, melted**
½ **teaspoon garlic powder**
2 cups buttermilk biscuit mix
⅔ **cup milk**
½ **cup shredded cheddar cheese**

Preheat the oven to 450 degrees. In a small bowl, combine the melted butter or margarine with the garlic powder. Set aside. In a large bowl, combine the biscuit mix, milk, and cheddar cheese. Beat the ingredients vigorously for about 30 seconds with a wooden spoon, until the mixture turns into a soft dough. Drop the dough by heaping tablespoons onto an ungreased cookie sheet. Bake the biscuits for 8–10 minutes, or until just golden brown. Before removing the biscuits from the oven, brush the garlic mixture on the tops. Serve warm.

Sesame Seed Wafers

Yield: 8 dozen wafers

These wafers are a great accompaniment for the Soul Food Dip on page 110.

¾ **cup vegetable or corn oil**
2 **cups firmly packed light brown sugar**
1 **egg**
1 **cup all-purpose flour**
½ **teaspoon baking powder**
¼ **teaspoon salt**
1 **teaspoon vanilla extract**
¾ **cup toasted sesame seeds (see page 129)**

Preheat the oven to 325 degrees. In a large bowl, combine the oil, brown sugar, and egg. Beat the ingredients until fluffy and well blended. Stir in the flour, baking powder, and salt. Mix well. Add the vanilla and sesame seeds.

Lightly grease a cookie sheet. Drop the dough, ½ teaspoon at a time, onto the cookie sheet. Bake for about 10 minutes, or until golden brown. Remove the sheet from the oven and allow the wafers to cool at least 2–3 minutes, to prevent breakage, before lifting them off. Repeat with remaining dough. Store the wafers in a covered container.

Liberian Pineapple Nut Bread

Yield: 1 loaf

Eighty-six African-Americans traveled to Liberia, West Africa, in 1820 to escape the hardships of slavery and to form a free black colony there. The citizens of Liberia overcame many hardships to emerge as a proud republic inhabited by free African-Americans in 1847. I've found that recipes from Liberia are a unique blend of African and African-American culinary traditions. This pineapple bread tastes even better the second day.

2½ cups all-purpose flour
1 tablespoon baking powder
1 teaspoon baking soda
1 teaspoon salt
1 cup wheat bran
2 eggs, beaten
¾ cup crushed pineapple, drained
½ cup chopped roasted peanuts or walnuts

Sift the flour, baking powder, baking soda, and salt into a large bowl. Mix in the wheat bran. Add the eggs, pineapple, and ¼ cup of the nuts. Mix together thoroughly. Pour the batter into a greased loaf pan. Bake for 1 hour, or until a toothpick or tester inserted in the middle of the loaf comes out clean. Sprinkle with the remaining chopped peanuts or walnuts.

✿ Toasting Seeds and Nuts

Seeds and nuts (whole or in pieces) can be toasted by placing them in a single layer on a cookie sheet in a 350 degree oven. They will cook quickly, so be careful not to let them burn. Bake the seeds or nuts for 2 minutes, then shake the cookie sheet so the seeds or nuts brown evenly. Bake for another 2–3 minutes, shaking the cookie sheet occasionally, until the seeds or nuts turn golden brown. Toasting seeds and nuts brings out their flavor and aroma.

Bacon Cornbread Muffins

Yield: 12 muffins

"Art is the material evidence that remains of the wealth of our culture—of who we are."

—MARY SCHMIDT CAMPBELL, NEW YORK CITY OFFICIAL

12 slices bacon
1 cup self-rising flour
1 cup self-rising yellow cornmeal
¼ cup sugar
2 eggs, well beaten
1 cup milk

Preheat the oven to 425 degrees. In a skillet, cook the bacon until crisp, then remove and drain on paper towels. Reserve ¼ cup of the bacon fat. In a large bowl, mix together the flour, cornmeal, and sugar. Add the beaten eggs, milk, and reserved bacon fat. Mix well. Crumble the bacon and add it to the cornmeal mixture. Lightly grease a 12-cup muffin pan. Spoon the cornmeal mixture into each cup until almost full. Bake for 20–25 minutes.

Monkey Bread

Yield: 8 servings

"Dream big dreams! Others may deprive you of your material wealth and cheat you in a thousand ways, but no man can deprive you of the control and use of your imagination."

—THE REVEREND JESSE JACKSON, PREACHER AND ACTIVIST

¼ **cup sugar**
1 **teaspoon ground cinnamon**
3 **8-ounce packages refrigerator biscuits, cut into quarters**

GLAZE:
1 **stick butter or margarine, melted**
1 **teaspoon ground cinnamon**
½ **cup sugar**

Preheat the oven to 350 degrees. In a small bowl, mix together the sugar and cinnamon. Separate the biscuits and dip each in the mixture until well coated. Set aside any remaining cinnamon mixture. In a buttered Bundt pan, layer the cinnamon-covered biscuits.

GLAZE:
Mix the melted butter or margarine with the cinnamon and sugar. Stir in any remaining cinnamon sugar from the biscuits. Mix well and spoon over the top of the biscuits. Bake for 30 minutes and serve warm.

Wheat Germ Muffins

Yield: 12 muffins

"I believe in helping people the best way you can; my way is through my art. But sometimes you need a splash of cold water in your face to make you see the right way to do it."

—ARTHUR MITCHELL,
FOUNDER OF THE DANCE THEATER OF HARLEM

1½ cups all-purpose flour
2 teaspoons baking powder
1 teaspoon salt
¼ cup sugar
1 cup wheat germ
½ stick butter or margarine, melted
¼ cup light molasses
1 egg, well beaten
¾ cup milk

Preheat the oven to 400 degrees. In a large bowl, mix the flour, baking powder, and salt. Add the sugar, wheat germ, butter or margarine, molasses, egg, and milk. Stir until all ingredients are well blended. Spoon the batter into a greased 12-cup muffin pan until each cup is almost full. Bake for 20 minutes.

West Indian Corn Pone

Yield: 1 loaf

Corn pone is sold in open-air craft markets in many places in the West Indies. The spices make this de-lightfully different from African-American corn pone. This is an excellent bread to serve with chicken or beef.

2 cups yellow cornmeal
½ cup all-purpose flour
2 teaspoons baking powder
½ teaspoon salt
1 cup sugar
¾ teaspoon ground nutmeg
¼ teaspoon ground allspice
1 cup milk
½ cup canned cream of coconut
½ cup raisins

Preheat the oven to 325 degrees. In a large bowl, com-bine the cornmeal, flour, baking powder, salt, sugar, nut-meg, and allspice. Add the milk and cream of coconut a little at a time, mixing well after each addition, until the ingredients are smoothly blended. Mix in the raisins. Pour into a greased 9-inch baking pan and bake for 20–25 minutes, until brown.

Kuumba Pie

Yield: 8 servings

I love this creative combination of white chocolate, almonds, and pecans!

4 eggs
1 cup light corn syrup
⅔ cup sugar
3 tablespoons butter, melted
1½ teaspoons vanilla extract
1½ teaspoons almond extract
1½ teaspoons chocolate extract
6 ounces white chocolate, melted (see note)
1 cup pecan halves
1 cup slivered almonds
1 unbaked 9-inch pie crust (see page 137)

Preheat the oven to 350 degrees. In the large bowl of an electric mixer, beat the eggs until fluffy. Add the rest of the ingredients except for the pecans, almonds, and pie crust. Beat until well blended, about 3 minutes. Stir in the pecans and almonds. Pour the mixture into the pie crust. Bake for 50–55 minutes, until set.

Note: To melt the chocolate, place it in a small heatproof bowl and set it in a pan of hot but not boiling water, or in the top of a double boiler over medium-low heat. Stir until the chocolate has melted.

Munchie Delight

Yield: 15 servings

I started making this dessert more than fifteen years ago and now I can't attend a family gathering without a pan of this cool, creamy confection in my hands. Oh well, I could be famous for something much more time-consuming than this easy-to-make delight!

CRUST:

1½ sticks butter or margarine, melted
1½ cups all-purpose flour
⅛ teaspoon salt
¾ cup finely chopped pecans or almonds

FILLING:

1 8-ounce package cream cheese
1 cup powdered sugar
1 13½-ounce carton frozen whipped topping

PUDDING:

2 3.9-ounce packages chocolate instant pudding mix
4 cups milk

GARNISHES:

1 8-ounce carton frozen whipped topping, thawed
⅓ cup chopped pecans or almonds
⅓ cup grated chocolate

Preheat the oven to 375 degrees. In a medium bowl, mix the melted butter or margarine with the flour, salt, and pecans or almonds. Press the flour mixture into the bottom of a 13 × 9 × 2-inch baking dish. Bake for 15 minutes, or until lightly browned. Remove from the oven and set aside until cool.

Using a mixer or food processor, combine the cream cheese, powdered sugar, and whipped topping until well blended. Set aside in the refrigerator. Make the chocolate pudding according to the package directions, with the milk. When the pudding has chilled and set, assemble the dessert by placing the whipped topping mixture on top of the crust. Spread the pudding on top. Cover with plastic wrap and refrigerate until serving time.

Serve the dessert directly from the pan, with a dollop of whipped topping sprinkled with chopped pecans or almonds and grated chocolate.

Old-fashioned Pie Crust

Yield: 2 9-inch pie crusts

2½ cups all-purpose flour
½ teaspoon salt
4 tablespoons shortening
1 stick cold butter or margarine
½ cup cold water, or as needed

In a large mixing bowl, combine the flour and salt. Cut in the shortening until the mixture is well blended. Slice the butter or margarine into small pieces. Rub or cut the pieces into the flour mixture until it resembles coarse cornmeal. Slowly add the water, a few tablespoons at a time. Using your hands, gently mix in the water until the mixture is moist and forms a dough. Do not knead the dough; it will make the pie crust tough. Form the dough into two equal-sized balls, wrap the balls in plastic wrap, and refrigerate for at least 30 minutes. Roll out each crust on a floured surface to ⅛ inch thick, then proceed according to any recipe instructions.

Almond-Granola Pie Crust

Yield: 1 9-inch pie crust

This healthy, nut-flavored pie crust is easy to make ahead of time. The Fruits of Africa filling on page 139 goes well with this crust.

½ cup ground almonds
½ cup rolled oats, granola, or muesli
1 cup whole-wheat pastry flour
1 teaspoon ground cinnamon
¼ teaspoon sea salt
1 stick cold unsalted butter
1½ tablespoons honey

In a large bowl, mix the almonds, oats, granola, or muesli, flour, cinnamon, and salt. Cut in the butter. Add the honey and gather the dough into a ball. Do not roll it out; instead, pinch off pieces and press them into the pie pan, starting from the center of the pan and pressing out to the edges of the pan. Cover the rim of the pan with the dough and pinch the edges into a design. Refrigerate the crust for at least 1–2 hours. Bake for 5 minutes at 350 degrees. Cool and fill.

Fruits of Africa Pie

Yield: 1 9-inch pie

"We must always use time creatively . . . and forever realize that the time is always ripe to do right."
—MARTIN LUTHER KING, JR.

1½ cups papaya, guava, or apricot nectar
4 tablespoons lemon juice
4 tablespoons sugar
½ teaspoon salt
4 tablespoons cornstarch
2 cups diced fresh fruit—papaya, pineapple, melon, oranges, guavas
Almond-Granola Pie Crust (see page 138) or 1 baked 9-inch pie crust (see note)

TOPPING:
1 cup heavy cream, whipped, or 1 8-ounce carton frozen whipped topping, thawed
½ cup shredded coconut
½ cup chopped peanuts

In a 2-quart saucepan, bring the nectar to a boil, then turn heat down to a simmer. In a small bowl, mix together the lemon juice, sugar, and salt. Slowly add the cornstarch, stirring well until smooth. Add the mixture to the nectar in the saucepan. Turn the heat to medium and cook, stirring constantly, until the glaze is thick and clear. Cool for 10 minutes, then add the 2 cups diced fruit, stirring until the pieces are well coated. Pour the filling into a cooked pie crust and refrigerate until chilled. Before serving, cover the pie with whipped cream or whipped topping. Garnish with coconut and chopped peanuts.

Note: Preheat the oven to 450 degrees. Prick the pie crust with a fork to release air while it is cooking. Bake crust for 15–18 minutes or until the crust is golden brown. Allow crust to cool before using.

Chocolate Chip Pie

Yield: 1 9-inch pie

"I am not a blues singer. I am not a jazz singer. I am not a country singer. But I am a singer who can sing the blues, who can sing jazz, who can sing country."

—RAY CHARLES, MUSICIAN

1 stick butter or margarine, softened
2 eggs
1 cup sugar
½ cup self-rising flour
1 teaspoon vanilla extract
½ teaspoon salt
1 cup broken pecans
1 6-ounce package chocolate chips
1 unbaked 9-inch pie crust (see page 137)

Preheat the oven to 350 degrees. In the large bowl of an electric mixer, on medium speed, combine the butter or margarine, eggs, sugar, flour, vanilla, and salt until well blended. Stir in the pecans by hand, gently mixing well, then the chocolate chips. Pour the mixture into an unbaked pie crust. Bake for 40–45 minutes.

Deep-Dish Apple Pie

Yield: 1 9-inch pie

This pie in a baking dish, with a pastry top, can be made very quickly by using canned apples and packaged pie dough. It can bake while you're eating dinner. Serve it hot, topped with vanilla ice cream, and you'll have a sweet ending for any meal.

8 cooking apples, peeled, cored, and sliced, or 2 20-ounce cans sliced apples
1½ cups sugar
3 tablespoons all-purpose flour
1½ teaspoons ground cinnamon
¼ teaspoon ground nutmeg
⅛ teaspoon salt
3 tablespoons butter or margarine
Dough to top 1 9-inch pie (see page 137)

Preheat the oven to 400 degrees. Arrange the apple slices in a lightly buttered 9-inch baking dish. In a medium bowl, mix the sugar, flour, cinnamon, nutmeg, and salt. Sprinkle the mixture over the apples and toss lightly. Then dot with butter or margarine. Top the apples with the uncooked pie crust. Make several slits in the crust to allow steam to escape. Bake for 40 minutes, or until the juice bubbles through and the crust is golden brown.

Southern Peanut Pie

Yield: 1 9-inch pie

"People ask where [the stories] come from—I don't know and I'm not bothering it, because if I keep bothering it I am not going to be able to do it."

—J. CALIFORNIA COOPER, AUTHOR

1 cup sugar
¾ cup light corn syrup
1 stick butter or margarine, melted
3 eggs
½ teaspoon vanilla extract
1½ cups roasted peanuts
1 unbaked 9-inch pie crust (see page 137)

Preheat the oven to 375 degrees. In the large bowl of an electric mixer, on medium speed, combine the sugar, corn syrup, butter or margarine, eggs, and vanilla until well blended. Turn off the mixer and stir in the peanuts. Pour the mixture into the pie crust. Bake for 45 minutes, or until set.

Sweet Potato and Pecan Pie

Yield: 6–8 servings

I had never heard of a pie like this one. But when I read the ingredients, my Southern roots began craving it right away.

2 cups peeled, thinly sliced sweet potatoes
1½ cups sugar
½ stick plus 2 tablespoons butter, melted
1 teaspoon ground nutmeg
1 teaspoon grated orange zest
½ cup finely chopped pecans
Dough for 2 unbaked 9-inch pie crusts (see page 137)

Preheat the oven to 350 degrees. In a large pot, drop the potato slices in just enough water to cover. Cook the potatoes about 10 minutes, or until tender. Remove from the heat. Retain the liquid. Gently stir in the sugar, the ½ stick butter, the nutmeg, orange zest, and pecans. Roll half the dough to a ⅛-inch thickness and line the bottom of a pie pan with it. Spoon in the potato mixture, along with the liquid. Roll out the remaining dough to a ⅛-inch thickness. Place the dough on top of the potatoes, pressing the edges to seal. Make several slits in the top of the crust to allow steam to escape and brush with the remaining 2 tablespoons melted butter. Bake the pie for 30 minutes, or until done.

Quick Cherry Cobbler

Yield: 6 servings

"I've always told the musicians in my band to play what they know and then play above that. Because then anything can happen, and that's where great art and music happens."

—MILES DAVIS, MUSICIAN

2 cups sugar
1 egg, beaten
½ cup milk
¾ cup self-rising flour
1 tablespoon butter or margarine, melted
1 16-ounce can tart red pitted cherries, undrained

Preheat the oven to 425 degrees. In the large bowl of an electric mixer, at medium speed, combine ½ cup of the sugar, the egg, milk, flour, and butter or margarine; mix well for about 3 minutes. Pour the mixture into a lightly greased 1½-quart baking dish. In a small saucepan, combine the remaining 1½ cups sugar and the cherries. Bring to a boil, stirring constantly to prevent sticking. Pour the cherry mixture on top of the flour mixture in the baking dish. Bake for 15–20 minutes, or until the top is brown. This cobbler makes its own crust.

Simple Pound Cake

Yield: 1 loaf

"Pictures just come to my mind and I tell my heart to go ahead."

—HORACE PIPPIN, ARTIST

2 sticks butter or margarine, softened
1¾ cups sugar
5 eggs
½ teaspoon almond extract
2 cups all-purpose flour

Preheat the oven to 350 degrees. Using an electric mixer at medium speed, cream the butter or margarine and sugar until fluffy. Add the eggs, one at a time, beating well after each addition. Add the almond extract. Sprinkle in the flour, a little at a time, and beat until the batter is well blended. Lightly grease and flour a 9 × 5 × 3-inch loaf pan. Spoon the batter into the pan and bake for 1 hour and 10 minutes, or until a tester inserted into the center of the cake comes out clean.

Chocolate Pound Cake

Yield: 1 10-inch cake

"The blues has been the foundation for all other American music since the beginning."

—WILLIE DIXON, MUSICIAN

2 sticks butter or margarine, softened
1½ cups sugar
4 eggs
8 1⅛-ounce milk chocolate candy bars, melted
1 cup buttermilk
2½ cups all-purpose flour
⅛ teaspoon salt
¼ teaspoon baking soda
1 5½-ounce can chocolate syrup
2 teaspoons vanilla extract
1 cup chopped pecans
Powdered sugar (optional)

Preheat the oven to 325 degrees. In the large bowl of an electric mixer, on medium speed, cream the butter or margarine and sugar until fluffy. Add the eggs, one at a time, mixing the batter well after each egg is added. Add the melted candy bars and the buttermilk; mix well.

In a small bowl, sift together the flour, salt, and baking soda. Gradually, on medium speed, add the flour mixture to the chocolate batter. Add the chocolate syrup and vanilla; mix well. Turn off the motor and stir in the pecans. Spoon the batter into a lightly greased and floured

10-inch tube pan or Bundt pan. Bake for 1¼ hours, or until a tester inserted into the center of the cake comes out clean. Allow the cake to cool and remove it from the Bundt or tube pan onto a cake plate or rack. Sprinkle with powdered sugar if desired when the cake is cool.

Pineapple Cake

Yield: 9–12 servings

I've heard many stories about "Mama's (or Grandma's) boiled topping pineapple cake." Some women told me that they even had a special pan, used only for this pineapple cake! I was very happy to discover this old recipe, and once you try it you'll be happy too.

CAKE:

2 eggs

2 cups sugar

2 cups all-purpose flour

2½ teaspoons baking powder

2 cups crushed pineapple, undrained

TOPPING:

1 cup sugar

1 5-ounce can evaporated milk

1 stick margarine

1 cup coarsely chopped pecans

1 cup shredded coconut

½ teaspoon vanilla extract

½ teaspoon lemon extract

Preheat the oven to 350 degrees. In the large bowl of an electric mixer, beat the eggs and sugar together at medium speed until fluffy. In a small bowl, sift the flour and baking powder together. Add the flour mixture to the egg mixture a little at a time, beating until the batter is smooth. Gently stir in the pineapple by hand.

Spoon the batter into a lightly greased and floured 9 × 13 × 2-inch baking dish. Bake for 25–30 minutes, until a tester inserted into the center comes out clean.

During the final minutes that the cake is baking, prepare the topping. In a medium saucepan, mix the sugar, milk, and margarine. Stirring constantly, heat until the margarine melts and the mixture boils. Boil for at least 2 minutes, stirring constantly. Remove the pan from the heat and add the pecans, coconut, and the vanilla and lemon extracts. When the cake is done, pour the topping over the hot cake immediately. You may want to return the cake to the oven for an additional 5–10 minutes to brown the coconut and pecans.

Simple Cheesecake

Yield: 6–8 servings

This cheesecake can be eaten as is or decorated with sliced fruit or canned pie filling. It's good no matter how you top it!

2 8-ounce packages cream cheese
3 eggs
¾ cup plus 3 tablespoons sugar
1½ teaspoons vanilla extract
1 cup sour cream

Preheat the oven to 350 degrees. In the large bowl of an electric mixer, combine the cream cheese, eggs, ¾ cup of the sugar, and ½ teaspoon of the vanilla. Beat for 3–5 minutes at medium speed. Pour the batter into a 9-inch pie pan that has been lightly greased with vegetable oil. Bake for 25 minutes. Cool at least 30 minutes. In a small bowl, combine the sour cream, the remaining sugar, and the remaining vanilla. Pour the topping over the cake and bake it another 10 minutes. Chill for at least 4 hours.

Luscious Lemon Sugar Cookies

Yield: 6 dozen cookies

"We see things not as they are, but as we are. Our perception is shaped by our previous experiences."

—DENNIS KIMBRO, AUTHOR

2 sticks butter or margarine, softened
1½ cups sugar
1 egg
⅓ cup frozen lemonade concentrate, thawed and undiluted
4 cups all-purpose flour
1 teaspoon baking powder
1 teaspoon baking soda
¼ teaspoon salt
½ cup buttermilk
2 tablespoons sugar
½ teaspoon ground nutmeg

Preheat the oven to 375 degrees. In the large bowl of an electric mixer, at medium speed, cream the butter or margarine and sugar until smooth. Add the egg and lemonade concentrate and continue beating at medium speed until fluffy. Sift the flour, baking powder, baking soda, and salt into a large bowl. Turn the mixer to low speed. Alternately, add the flour mixture and the buttermilk, a little at a time, to the lemonade mixture until the ingredients are thoroughly blended. On an ungreased cookie sheet, drop teaspoons of the cookie dough, spacing the rows apart evenly.

In a small bowl, combine the 2 tablespoons sugar and the nutmeg. Wet the bottom of a glass in water. Dip the wet glass into the sugar mixture. Flatten the cookies with the bottom of the sugar-coated glass, rewetting and recoating the bottom of the glass after each cookie. Bake the cookies, in batches, for 10–12 minutes, or until golden brown.

Chocolate Nut Squares

Yield: 48 squares

"In my writing, as much as I could, I tried to find the good, and praise it."

—ALEX HALEY, AUTHOR

1 cup light brown sugar, packed
2 sticks margarine or butter, softened
1½ teaspoons vanilla extract
1 egg
2 cups all-purpose flour
½ cup light corn syrup
2 tablespoons margarine or butter
1 12-ounce package semisweet chocolate chips
1 12-ounce can salted mixed nuts

Preheat the oven to 350 degrees. In the large bowl of an electric mixer, combine the brown sugar, margarine or butter, vanilla, and egg at medium speed until well blended. Gradually add the flour, still beating at medium speed. Spread the batter on the bottom of an ungreased 13 × 9 × 2-inch baking dish. Bake for 20 minutes, or until lightly browned. Cool.

In a small saucepan, heat the corn syrup, 2 tablespoons margarine or butter, and the chocolate chips over low heat. Stir constantly until the chips are melted. Cool.

Spread this chocolate mixture over the cake in the baking dish. Sprinkle with the nuts and gently press them into the chocolate. Refrigerate, uncovered, until the chocolate is firm, about 2 hours. Cut into 2-inch squares.

Peanut Butter Bars

Yield: 32 bars

"We get closer to God as we get more intimately and understandingly acquainted with the things He has created. I know of nothing more inspiring than that of making discoveries for one's self."

—GEORGE WASHINGTON CARVER,
SCIENTIST AND EDUCATOR

1 cup all-purpose flour
½ cup sugar
½ cup firmly packed light brown sugar
½ teaspoon baking soda
¼ teaspoon salt
1 stick butter or margarine, softened
⅓ cup and ¼ cup crunchy peanut butter
1 egg
1 cup uncooked oats (not instant)
1 12-ounce package semisweet chocolate chips
½ cup sifted powdered sugar
2–4 tablespoons milk

In the large bowl of an electric mixer, combine the flour, sugars, baking soda, salt, butter or margarine, ⅓ cup of the peanut butter, the egg, and the oats; mix well at medium speed. Press the dough into a lightly greased 13 × 9 × 2-inch baking dish and bake for 20 minutes. Sprinkle the chocolate chips over the hot cake. When the chips begin to melt, spread the chocolate evenly.

In a small bowl, combine the powdered sugar, the remaining ¼ cup peanut butter, and the milk. Beat until well blended. Drizzle the peanut butter mixture over the cake. Cool and cut into bars.

Walnut-Raisin Squares

Yield: 20 squares

"There is no such thing that 'all blacks have rhythm.' It's not that they're born with rhythm, but in black homes you always hear music. It becomes instinctive, a lot rubs off."

—ARTHUR MITCHELL,
FOUNDER OF THE DANCE THEATER OF HARLEM

2 cups raisins
1 cup walnuts
¼ cup sweetened condensed milk
2 tablespoons butter or margarine
½ cup powdered sugar

Place the raisins and walnuts in a food processor or blender. Grind until ingredients are finely chopped. In a small bowl, combine the milk and raisin mixture well. Using the 2 tablespoons butter or margarine, grease an 8-inch pan. Sprinkle half the powdered sugar over the butter. Press the raisin mixture into the sugar. Sprinkle the remaining powdered sugar over the top. Chill at least 2 hours and then cut into squares.

Butterscotch Cookies

Yield: 3 dozen squares

"I don't think there is anything in the world I can't do. . . . In my creative source, whatever that is, I don't see why I can't sculpt. Why shouldn't I? Human beings sculpt. I'm a human being."

—MAYA ANGELOU, AUTHOR AND POET

1 stick butter
2 cups light-brown sugar
2 eggs
1 teaspoon vanilla extract
2 cups all-purpose flour
2 teaspoons baking powder
¼ teaspoon salt
1 cup shredded coconut
½ cup chopped walnuts

Preheat the oven to 350 degrees. In a medium saucepan, melt the butter and sugar over low heat, stirring constantly, until bubbly. Remove the pan from the heat and cool. Add the eggs to the pan, one at a time, beating thoroughly with a whisk after each addition. Add the vanilla and stir well. Sift the flour, baking powder, and salt into a medium bowl. Add the flour mixture, a cup at a time, to the butter-sugar mixture, stirring well after each addition. Stir in the coconut and walnuts. Spread the cookie dough over the bottom of a greased 13 × 9 × 2-inch baking dish. Bake about 25 minutes, or until brown. While the cookies are still warm, cut them into squares. Cool and store in an airtight container.

Candy Cookies

Yield: 5–6 dozen cookies

These delicious cookies require little effort and no baking! A perfect treat for the holidays.

2 cups sugar
½ cup milk
⅓ cup cocoa
1 stick butter or margarine
½ cup crunchy peanut butter
1 teaspoon vanilla extract
3 cups instant oats

In a large saucepan over medium heat, mix the sugar, milk, cocoa, and butter or margarine. Stirring constantly, cook the mixture until it comes to a boil. Remove the pan from the heat. Add the peanut butter, vanilla, and oats; stir well. Place waxed paper on an ungreased cookie sheet. Drop teaspoons of the cookie batter onto the waxed paper. Let the cookies cool—do not bake them. Place the cookies in an airtight container.

Chocolate Peanut Chill

Yield: 12 servings

This dessert brings any Kwanzaa feast to a sweet conclusion.

2 cups chocolate wafer crumbs (from about 36 wafers)
⅓ cup margarine or butter, melted
¼ cup sugar
1 cup chopped peanuts
1 cup chocolate fudge topping
½ cup caramel-flavored topping
1 half-gallon block vanilla ice cream

In a small bowl, mix together the wafer crumbs, melted margarine or butter, and sugar. Using an ungreased, 9-inch-square baking pan, press the mixture firmly into the bottom. In a medium bowl, mix the peanuts, ½ cup of the fudge topping, and all of the caramel-flavored topping. Spread over the crumb mixture. Remove the ice cream from the package and cut it crosswise into 2-inch-thick slices. Lay the slices on top of the peanut mixture. Set aside until the ice cream has softened. Then, spread the ice cream evenly over the peanut mixture. Drizzle with the remaining ½ cup fudge topping. Cover with plastic wrap and freeze for at least 12 hours before serving.

7

Gifts from the Kitchen

IMANI
(Faith)
To believe with all our heart in our people, our parents, our
teachers, our leaders, and the righteousness and victory of
our struggle for a new and better world.

The Bible says that faith is "a gift of God." I believe that.
It would take God to create something as wonderful and
life-sustaining as faith. It takes a great faith to continue
on in the midst of all the troubles we face day in and day
out. The wonderful thing about faith is that the more you
use it, the more it grows. Unlike earthly things, which
become worn and depleted when used time after time,
faith becomes even stronger and more abundant the
more you use it.

Many times I've heard about people "losing faith." I've
discovered that things lost can be found in the most unexpected places at the most unexpected times, often
when I'm looking for something else. What I'd thought

I'd lost was there all the time, waiting for me to discover it again. Faith is like that. Sometimes when you think you've reached the end of your ability to believe, something or someone comes along to shore you up so that you can continue on.

I have great faith in the future and abilities of the African-American community. We must love and speak lovingly about our community. What is not loved will not grow properly. We must have faith in our personal abilities and in our potential as a people in order to grow.

The Reverend Cornel West says that "the major enemy of black survival in America is neither oppression nor exploitation but rather the nihilistic threat—that is, loss of hope and absence of meaning. For as long as hope remains and meaning is preserved, the possibility of overcoming oppression stays alive."

Hold on to hope, preserve meaning, and keep the faith.

Popcorn Nut Crunch

Yield: 2 pounds

A great *zawadi* gift is a decorated container filled with flavored popcorn and a videocassette of an African-American movie. These popcorn recipes are simple to prepare and make viewing the movie even more fun.

2 quarts popped corn
1⅓ cups pecan halves
⅔ cup almond slivers
2 sticks butter or margarine
1⅓ cups sugar
½ cup light corn syrup
1 teaspoon vanilla extract

In a large bowl, mix the popped corn, pecans, and almonds. In a medium saucepan, melt the butter or margarine over medium heat. Stir in the sugar and corn syrup; bring the mixture to a boil. Turn the heat down to low and, stirring occasionally, cook 10–15 minutes, or until the mixture turns a light caramel color. Remove the syrup from the heat and stir in the vanilla. Immediately pour the syrup over the popped corn mixture. Stir well to coat the ingredients evenly. On an ungreased cookie sheet, spread the mixture out evenly. When the coated popcorn is cool, break it apart into small pieces. Store the popcorn in an airtight container in a cool, dry place. It will keep three to four days.

Quick and Easy Caramel Corn

Yield: 4 quarts

This is a wonderful recipe for children to prepare and give as *zawadi* gifts. Clean-up is quick and easy too!

1 cup firmly packed light brown sugar
¼ cup light corn syrup
½ teaspoon salt
1½ tablespoons butter or margarine, cut up
½ teaspoon baking soda
3–4 quarts popped corn

In a medium microwavable bowl, combine the sugar, corn syrup, salt, and butter or margarine. Microwave on high for 1 minute, or until the butter or margarine has melted. Stir. Cook on high 2 more minutes. Stir in the baking soda, mixing well (baking soda may cause mixture to foam). Place the popped corn in a large brown paper bag. Pour the syrup over the corn. Close the bag and shake until the corn is well coated. Place the bag in the microwave oven and cook 1½ minutes more. On ungreased cookie sheets, spread out the popped corn to cool. Store in an airtight container in a cool, dry place. It will keep three to four days.

Pumpkin Cake in a Jar

Yield: 8 cakes

Use canning jars to bake this unusual recipe. Wrap a piece of colorful African wrapping paper around the lid and tie a piece of black, red, or green ribbon around the neck of the jar. This makes a tasty *za-wadi* gift!

⅔ **cup vegetable shortening**
2⅔ **cups sugar**
4 **eggs**
2 **cups puréed pumpkin, canned or fresh (boil before puréeing)**
⅔ **cup water**
3⅓ **cups all-purpose flour**
½ **teaspoon baking powder**
1½ **teaspoons salt**
1 **teaspoon ground cloves**
1 **teaspoon allspice**
2 **teaspoons baking soda**
1 **cup chopped pecans**

Preheat the oven to 350 degrees. Lightly grease 8 wide-mouth 1-pint ovenproof jars. In a large mixing bowl, cream the shortening and sugar. Beat in the eggs, one at a time, then the pumpkin and water. In a medium bowl, sift together the flour, baking powder, salt, spices, and baking soda. Add the dry ingredients, in batches, to the pumpkin batter, stirring well. Stir in the nuts.

Pour the batter into the jars until they are half full. Place the jars on a cookie sheet and bake upright for 45 minutes. The cakes will pull away from the sides of the jars. Remove the jars and cookie sheet from the oven. After the jars have cooled somewhat but are still warm, cover the top of each jar with a circle of waxed paper. Screw the lids on the jars and refrigerate. The cakes will slide out easily when it is time to serve them.

❖ Herbal Vinegars

Herbal vinegars are a wonderful gift from the kitchen. They are delicious when sprinkled on salads, vegetables, or broiled meats. Fruit vinegars bring out the flavors of fresh fruit salads or desserts. You can use either fresh or dried herbs or fresh or frozen fruit when preparing the vinegars. Pouring heated vinegar over herbs that have been slightly crushed helps to extract the flavor of the herbs. Almost any type of vinegar with at least 5 percent acidity may be used, except malt vinegar. The flavor of malt vinegar is too strong to blend well with herbs or fruits.

After preparation, herbal vinegars should be stored for 1 to 3 weeks in a cool, dark place to allow the flavors to mingle. Herbal vinegars will keep indefinitely. Do not make herbal oils at home, however. Unlike commercial oils, homemade herbal oils lack the acidity to preserve them; they tend to turn rancid and may cause botulism.

Decorative bottles like those used for wine or bottled water are perfect containers for your herbal vinegars. Sterilize the bottles or jars with boiling water before using them. Line the bottle caps or jar lids with a piece of aluminum foil, or place a piece of it over the mouth of the jar or bottle to prevent the cap from rusting. Bottles with a cork or cruets are also perfect containers. Place a decorative label describing the herbal ingredients on the bottle or jar. Containers may be decorated by tying a raffia bow, a few dried herb sprigs, or some dried flowers around the neck of the bottle or jar. Wrapping strands of brightly colored yarn or strips of Afrocentric wrapping paper dipped in glue would also add a decorative touch.

Herbal Vinegar

Yield: 2 cups

"As I grow older, part of my emotional survival plan must be to actively seek inspiration instead of passively waiting for it to find me."

—BEBE MOORE CAMPBELL, AUTHOR

4–6 tablespoons fresh or dried herbs (tarragon, chives, basil, marjoram, dill, sage, rosemary, savory, mustard, or bay leaves, in combination or alone)
2 cups vinegar (distilled white, cider, or red wine)

If using fresh herbs, rinse them and pat them dry with a paper towel. Bruise the herbs by rolling over them once or twice with a rolling pin. Place the herbs in a glass jar that has been boiled to sterilize it. In a small non-corrosive saucepan, heat the vinegar until it is warm to the touch but not hot. If using a microwave oven, place the vinegar in a glass bowl and heat on low power about 30 seconds. Pour the vinegar over the herbs and let the mixture cool. Place a piece of aluminum foil either over the mouth of the jar or around the cap and seal the jar tightly. Label the jar and put the herbal vinegar in a cool, dark place for at least 1–3 weeks so that the flavors have a chance to mingle. Shake the mixture every other day. After the vinegar has been infused, place several layers of cheesecloth inside a funnel and strain the vinegar into a sterilized bottle or jar. Discard the herbs, as the flavors have been rendered. You may want to place a sprig of fresh herbs inside the bottle or jar. Leave at least 1 inch free at the top of the bottle if inserting a cork or glass stopper.

Spicy Vinegar

Yield: 2 cups

"When things got bad, I'd sing 'Ave Maria,' which
is one of my favorite songs from childhood . . . it
was my salvation. It gave me a reason to believe
that things would change."

—AARON NEVILLE, SINGER

2 cups fresh green or red chili peppers (see page 33)
2 cups white wine vinegar
4 cloves garlic, sliced
4–5 whole black peppercorns
3–4 fresh green chili peppers (jalapeño or Anaheim)
 for decoration

In a large saucepan, scald the 2 cups peppers in boiling
water for 1 minute. Immediately drain and rinse the peppers under cold running water. Set aside until cool. In a
small non-corrosive saucepan, heat the vinegar until it is
warm to the touch, not hot. If using a microwave oven,
pour the vinegar into a glass bowl. Heat on low power for
about 30–45 seconds. Place the garlic, peppercorns, and
blanched chilies in a glass bowl. Pour the vinegar over
the chili mixture and let it cool. Then pour the spicy vinegar through a funnel into a glass jar that has been
boiled to sterilize it. Place a piece of foil over the mouth
of the jar or around the cap and seal the jar tightly. Label
the jar and put the vinegar in a cool, dark place for at

least 1–3 weeks so that the flavors have a chance to mingle. Shake the mixture every other day. After the vinegar has been infused, strain it into a sterilized bottle or jar and discard solids. Wash and pat dry 1 or 2 large fresh chilies or several small ones and place them on a wooden skewer in the bottle or jar for decoration.

Fruit Vinegar

Yield: 1 quart

"It's true that when God closes a door He always opens a window. Trouble is, some folks refuse to crawl through the window. It doesn't matter how you get into the house as long as you're there to open the door when opportunity knocks."

—ANGELA SHELF MEDEARIS

1 quart white wine or cider vinegar
2 cups fresh or frozen cherries, cranberries, blackberries, blueberries, or strawberries—alone or any combination
½ cup light clover honey
4 whole cloves
4 cinnamon sticks, broken into 3-inch pieces

In a medium non-corrosive saucepan, combine the vinegar and 1 cup of the berries (if frozen, thaw and rinse off the syrup). Over high heat, bring the mixture to a boil. Lower the heat immediately and simmer, uncovered, for 2 minutes. Stir in the honey and remove the pan from the heat. Strain the mixture through a fine-mesh strainer into a clean bowl. Do not press on the berries. Discard the solids.

Place the remaining berries, cloves, and cinnamon sticks in equal amounts in a 32-ounce bottle, 2 16-ounce bottles, or 4 8-ounce bottles (any container should be sterilized by boiling first). Leave at least 1 inch free at the top of the bottle if inserting a cork or glass stopper. Label the jar and place the vinegar in a cool, dark place for at least 1–3 weeks so that the flavors have a chance to mingle. Shake the mixture every other day.

❖ Sachets and Potpourri

Sachets and potpourri make beautiful and aromatic *zawadi* gifts. Sachets can be made of a variety of herbs or potpourri and are simple to make. The bath sachets may be placed directly into the tub or tied to the faucet so that the hot water passes through the herbal mixture as the bath is drawn. Sachet bags may also be placed inside clothes drawers, tucked into the corners of couches or armchairs, or placed inside closets.

Any number of creative combinations may be used to make potpourri. Spices, flowers, essential oils, your favorite perfume, dried herbs, and citrus peels all make a wonderful potpourri. Using a fixative, such as tincture of benzoin, styrax, orris root, or muskene, will extend the life of the perfume and ingredients. Most fixatives can be purchased at craft stores.

Bath Sachets

Yield: 8 bath sachets

" 'For God so loved the world that He gave His only begotten Son, that whosoever believeth in Him should not perish, but have everlasting life.' These words stored up a battery of faith and confidence and determination in my heart which has not failed me to this day."

—MARY McLEOD BETHUNE,
EDUCATOR AND REFORMER

2 cups dried herbs (lavender, sage, rosemary, pennyroyal, lemon verbena, camomile, thyme, or mint—alone or in any combination)
8 4-inch squares cheesecloth or cotton (8 small handkerchiefs work well)
8 12-inch lengths ribbon or lace

Place the herbs in a plastic bag. Roll a rolling pin back and forth over the herbs until they are slightly crushed. Place ¼ cup of the dried herbs in the center of the cloth square. Gather the square in a pouf and knot a piece of ribbon or lace around the neck of the pouf to secure the herbs. Make the ribbon or lace into a bow, leaving the ends long enough to tie the bath sachet to a faucet.

Rose Petal Potpourri

Yield: 6 cups

"Let's not get too full of ourselves. Let's leave space
for God to come into the room."

−QUINCY JONES,
COMPOSER AND MUSICIAN

3 cups dried rose petals
2 cups dried lavender
1 cup dried lemon verbena
1 tablespoon dried lemon peel
1 tablespoon ground allspice
1 tablespoon ground cinnamon
1 tablespoon whole cloves
1½ tablespoons orris root

In a large jar, combine the rose petals and lavender. In a
medium bowl, mix the lemon verbena, lemon peel, allspice, cinnamon, cloves, and orris root. Pour the lemon
mixture into the jar containing the rose petals and lavender. Cover the jar tightly and shake the ingredients. Let
the potpourri stand for 4–6 weeks, shaking the mixture
frequently to combine the scents. Then divide it into
bowls to scent your rooms. It will give off a lovely scent
for months. Or place potpourri in a decorative bag and
give it as a gift.

Herbal Rubbing Lotion

Yield: 2 cups

This refreshing herbal lotion is a wonderful pick-me-up for sore muscles and tired minds at the end of a long day. The herbs also give the rubbing alcohol a pleasant fragrance. The herbs may be obtained from nurseries or grocery stores.

1 cup fresh lavender leaves
¼ cup lemon verbena leaves
¼ cup mint leaves
¼ cup rosemary sprigs
2 cups unscented rubbing alcohol

Place the herbs in a plastic bag. Roll a rolling pin back and forth over the herbs until they are slightly crushed. Place the herbs in a glass jar that has been sterilized by boiling. Add the rubbing alcohol. Cover tightly and label the jar NOT TO BE USED INTERNALLY. Set aside in a cool, dry place for 7–10 days. Strain the alcohol through several layers of cheesecloth into pretty jars or bottles. Cap tightly and label bottles or jars NOT TO BE USED INTERNALLY.

KWANZAA/SWAHILI PRONUNCIATION GUIDE AND GLOSSARY

Swahili is one of the most popular languages on the continent of Africa. Although the dialect is different from country to country, more than 45 million people in eastern Africa, and in most of Kenya, Tanzania, Rwanda, Burundi, Zambia, and Somalia speak a form of Swahili.

The proper name for Swahili is Kiswahili. The prefix (ki) is a definition of the actual language as opposed to the people who speak the language. For example, a person speaking Swahili would refer to the language spoken by the Ganda people as Kiganda.

There are only 24 letters in the Swahili alphabet. There is no sound for Q or X in the language. Swahili vowels are pronounced as follows:

> *a* is pronounced like the *a* in far
> *e* is pronounced like the *a* in say
> *i* is pronounced like the *ee* in see
> *o* is pronounced like the *oe* in toe
> *u* is pronounced like the *oo* in coo

Swahili consonants are pronounced the same way consonants are pronounced in English. *G* has a hard sound, as in *give*. *R* is like the Spanish *r* and is made by rolling the tongue. Place the accent on the next-to-last syllable in most Swahili words, unless otherwise indicated.

BENDERA (ben-de-ra): National black liberation flag. The *bendera* is black, red, and green and is similar to one that was first made popular by Marcus Garvey, founder and leader of the Universal Negro Improvement Association. Black is for the color of the people, red is for the struggle that is carried on by Africans and African-Americans for a better life, and green is for the future that will result from the struggle.

HABARI GANI (ha-ba-ri ga-ni): A Swahili phrase that means "What news?"

HARAMBEE (ha-ram-be): A Swahili word that means "Let's all pull together!"

IMANI (i-ma-ni): One of the seven principles of Kwanzaa. It means "faith" in Swahili.

KARAMU (ka-ra-mu): This is the Kwanzaa feast held on the evening of December 31.

KIKOMBE CHA UMOJA (ki-kom-be cha u-mo-ja): Unity cup. This cup is passed in honor of the family ancestors, and as a sign of unity.

KINARA (ki-na-ra): Candle holder. A symbol of our African ancestors, the root from which our families and people evolved.

KUCHUNGUZA TENA NA KUTOA AHADI TENA (ku-chu-ngu-za te-na na ku-toa a-ha-di te-na): The speech that helps the audience to remember Kwanzaa.

KUJICHAGULIA (ku-ji-cha-gu-lia): One of the seven principles of Kwanzaa. It means "self-determination" in Swahili.

KUKARIBISHA (ku-kar-i-bi-sha): The welcoming ceremony that is held at the beginning of the *karamu* feast.

KUKUMBUKA (ku-kum-bu-ka): A short speech by a member of the audience on the meaning of a Kwanzaa principle.

KUSHANGILIA (ku-shan-gi-lia): Rejoicing.

KUTOA MAJINA (ku-toa ma-ji-na): The calling of the names of the family ancestors, as well as African-American heroes and heroines.

KUUMBA (ku-um-ba): One of the seven principles of Kwanzaa. It means "creativity" in Swahili.

KWANZA (kwan-za): Means "first fruits" in Swahili.

KWANZAA (kwan-za): The African-American cultural holiday created in 1966 by Dr. Maulana Karenga.

KWANZAA YENU IWE NA HERI (kwan-za ye-nu i-we na he-ri): A greeting in Swahili that means "May y'all's Kwanzaa be with happiness."

LIBATION STATEMENT: The speech that is made

before passing the communal unity cup *(kikombe cha umoja)*.

MAZAO (ma-za-o): During the Kwanzaa celebration, a bowl of fruit and vegetables is placed on a mat, the *mkeka,* to represent the rewards of working together and the traditional harvest festival.

MISHUMAA SABA (mi-shu-ma-a sa-ba): The seven candles. Three red, one black, and three green are placed in the *kinara.* The black candle is always in the center. Each candle represents one of the seven principles, *nguzo saba,* of Kwanzaa.

MKEKA (m-ke-ka): Mat. The *mkeka* is a symbol for unity and represents a firm foundation to build on. All the symbols of Kwanzaa are placed on the *mkeka.*

NGOMA (n-go-ma): The drum performance given during the *karamu* feast.

NGUZO SABA (n-gu-zo sa-ba): A term that means "seven principles" in Swahili. The *nguzo saba* are the guides for daily living. This guide is studied during Kwanzaa, to be practiced throughout the year.

NIA (ni-a): One of the seven principles of Kwanzaa. It means "purpose" in Swahili.

SWAHILI (swa-hi-li): A nontribal African language used in many parts of Africa.

TAMSHI LA TAMBIKO (tam-shi la tam-bi-ko): The libation speech that is read before passing the unity cup.

TAMSHI LA TUTAONANA (tam-shi la tu-ta-o-na-na): The farewell speech that is given at the end of the *karamu* feast.

UJAMAA (u-ja-ma): One of the seven principles of Kwanzaa. It means "cooperative economics" in Swahili.

UJIMA (u-ji-ma): One of the seven principles of Kwanzaa. It means "collective work and responsibility" in Swahili.

UMOJA (u-mo-ja): One of the seven principles of Kwanzaa. It means "unity" in Swahili.

VIBUNZI (vi-bun-zi): The ears of corn that are used during Kwanzaa to represent children. Also known as Muhindi.

ZAWADI (za-wa-di): The gifts given during Kwanzaa as a reward for the commitments made and kept during the holiday and the past year.

Index